THE LIBRARY OF
THE COLLEGE OF WILLIAM AND MARY
IN VIRGINIA, 1693–1793

The Library of

The College of William and Mary

in Virginia, 1693–1793

JOHN M. *elville* JENNINGS

Published for
the Earl Gregg Swem Library of
The College of William and Mary in Virginia

———

The University Press of Virginia
Charlottesville

Library Contributions No. 6

Copyright © 1968 by the Earl Gregg Swem Library of
The College of William and Mary in Virginia

The University Press of Virginia

First published 1968

Library of Congress Catalog Card Number: 68–59130
Printed in the United States of America

Acknowledgments

T HE Earl Gregg Swem Library of The College of
William and Mary in Virginia is pleased to publish
this record of its beginnings in commemoration of the college's 275th year.

Two persons are primarily responsible for the publication. The project could not have been undertaken without the generous assistance of Frances Lois Willoughby,
M.D. Dr. Willoughby's gift was made in memory of her
brother, Edwin Eliott Willoughby, professor of library
science at the college from 1932 to 1935 and then chief
bibliographer at the Folger Shakespeare Library until his
death in 1959. With typical graciousness, John Melville
Jennings, Director of the Virginia Historical Society,
permitted use of his manuscript and, moreover, devoted
much time and thought to its preparation for publication.
The Swem Library is deeply indebted to them both.

William C. Pollard
Librarian

Williamsburg, Virginia
September 1968

Introduction

THIS inquiry into the book collections, financing, and management of the library of the College of William and Mary during the first one hundred years of its existence was originally undertaken at the suggestion of a formidable mentor and beloved friend, the late Earl Gregg Swem, William and Mary's librarian from 1920 to 1944. His name is fittingly applied to the building that now houses the research collections of the college. The findings were organized in monographic form in 1948, at which time the author benefited greatly from suggestions made by Dr. Swem, who was then very much alive, and by Drs. Ernst Posner and Arthur A. Ekirch of American University, under whom the writer was engaged in graduate studies.

A copy of the typewritten monograph was duly filed in the William and Mary library. There it reposed until May 1968, when William C. Pollard, Librarian of the Earl Gregg Swem Library, resolved to usher the text into print in partial observance of the 275th anniversary of the founding of the college. Apprised of these plans, the author, though agreeable to Mr. Pollard's resolution, prudently scanned the monograph for the first time since he

Contents

Illustrations

Illustrations

CHAPTER ONE

The Founding of the College
1617–1693

THE origins of the College of William and Mary and its library are imbedded in early seventeenth-century efforts to establish and maintain a seat of higher learning at Henrico, Virginia.[1] The impulse behind the initial but unsuccessful venture stemmed from a pious concern in England over the spiritual well-being of the American Indians. James I, in efforts to advance the Anglican faith, directed his clergy in 1617 to solicit funds for erecting a missionary college to propagate the gospel among the "savages." Fifteen hundred pounds collected under the royal auspices were turned over to the Virginia Company of London. The Virginia Company itself sought to promote the undertaking, ordering in 1618 that ten thousand acres of land within the Corporation of Henrico be set aside as an endowment for the proposed establishment.

The project, "being a waighty busines," was entrusted to a board on which the distinguished scholar and treasurer of the Virginia Company, Sir Edwin Sandys, served as an ex-officio member. On Sandys's recommendation, the board resolved to send tenants to cultivate the college lands and thus furnish the projected seat of learning with a regular income. Robert Rich, Puritan earl of Warwick, also interested in the undertaking, suggested that one of his followers, Captain William Weldon, be appointed to supervise the tenants. In consequence, fifty men under Weldon's direction were dispatched to Virginia. But faulty management and a failure properly to seat the college lands led to controversy and general dissatisfaction. Sir Edwin Sandys therefore engaged George Thorpe, a gentleman of King James's Privy Chamber, to go to Virginia as the company's deputy in managing the property. Affronted by this reflection on his administrative capabilities, Captain Weldon returned to England, where he was subsequently prosecuted for his failure to augment "the sacred Treasure of the Colledge for wch the Companie are to be accountable."[2]

In the meantime Rev. Patrick Copeland, presumably at the instigation of Governor Sir Thomas Dale, grew interested in the establishment of a public free school for the colony.[3] A committee appointed by the Virginia Company to examine the proposition decided that

a Collegiate or free-school should have dependence upon the Colledge in Virginia wch should be made capable to receave Scholars from the Schoole into such Scollerships and fellowshipps as the said Colledge shalbe endowed withall for the advancement of Schollers as they arise by degres and deserts in learninge.[4]

The name East India was given to the school inasmuch as Copeland secured the original funds for the project from members of the East India Company. And a site near Henrico was selected in the Corporation of Charles City.

The East India School Committee, composed of shrewd businessmen, recommended that the Virginia planters themselves be solicited for financial support, noting that the children of those adventurers would reap the greatest benefits from the undertaking. Indeed, a telling argument offered in favor of the school emphasized that the colonists had "been hitherto constrained to their great costs to send their children from thence hither [to England] to be taught."[5] The recommendations were accepted in 1621 when the Virginia Company confirmed the committee's report. The company agreed also to a proposal that one thousand acres of land be set aside as an endowment for the better maintenance of the schoolmaster and usher.

In short, the East India School in Charles City was conceived as a preparatory school for the youth of the colony and more especially for those anticipating advanced instruction at the Henrico establishment. This indicates that the university was planned not only as a missionary college for Indians but also as a seat of higher learning for the youth of the colony.

The Henrico project launched the first college library undertaken in British North America.[6] At a meeting of the quarter court of the Virginia Company held November 15, 1620 (old style),

a straunger stept in presentinge a Mapp of Sr Walter Rawlighes conteyninge a Descripcon of Guiana, and wth the same fower great books as the guifte of one vnto the Company that desyred his name might not be made knowne . . . wch books [were for] the Colledge in Virginia.[7]

The four great books were copies of William ("Painful") Perkins' newly corrected and amended *Workes*, in three volumes folio, and an English translation of St. Augustine's *De civitate Dei*. The same anonymous benefactor subsequently donated "a large Church Bible, the Cõmon prayer booke, Vrsinus Catichisme [that is, Zacharias Ursinus' *Summe of Christian religion*] and a smale Bible richly imbroydered."[8] He specified that the volumes were to be "sent to the Colledge in Virginia there to remaine in safftie to the vse of the Collegiates hereafter, and not suffered att any time to be sent abroade, or used in the meane while."[9]

Such a precedent perhaps inspired Rev. Thomas Bargrave, rector of Henrico parish, to leave his library to the proposed university upon his death in Virginia in 1621.[10] Bargrave, a nephew of the dean of Canterbury, was a Cambridge graduate, holding multiple degrees of bachelor of arts, master of arts, bachelor of divinity, and doctor of divinity.[11] His private library presumably reflected his scholarly training and pursuits. It was valued at one hundred marks, or roughly seventy pounds, which suggests that it was sizable. But the titles are not revealed in the surviving records. And, alas, the bequest failed to bring the donor that lasting fame and honor which a similar bequest, some eighteen years later, brought to John Harvard in New England. Bargrave nevertheless earned for himself the handsome distinction of being the first resident benefactor of an institutional library in British North America. The fact that the institution itself miscarried during the course of organization does not detract in the slightest from his high intentions.

By 1622 the projected seat of higher learning seemed headed for success. It possessed, among other endowments, the nucleus of a library. But in 1622 the venture suffered a catastrophic reverse. On Good Friday morning, March 22, the Indians, unimpressed by the spiritual vine planted in their midst, executed a skillfully conceived attack on the English settlements and completely wiped out the town of Henrico. Virtually all of the tenants on the college lands were massacred, including Deputy Thorpe.[12] Steps were immediately taken by the Virginia Company to resuscitate the project. But a more lethal blow was dealt in 1624 with the revocation of the charter of the Virginia Company. The colony thereupon became a royal province, and the Henrico plans were permitted to collapse.

The fate of the Henrico library collections cannot be ascertained. Lady Yeardley, widow of the earlier governor, delivered to the governor and Council in 1627 certain of the books that had been donated in 1619 by the anonymous English friend of the project.[13] The surviving records do not report the final disposition of those materials. The Bargrave collection was destroyed, in all probability, when the Indians fired the plantations.

In 1624 Edward Palmer, uncle of the unfortunate poet Sir Thomas Overbury, left all his lands and tenements in Virginia and New England for "the foundinge of maintenance of a universitie, and such schooles in Virginia as shall there be erected and shall be called *Academia Virginiensis et Oxoniensis*."[14] The bequest was conditioned on a failure of heirs in a line of descent within Palmer's family. Under the somewhat strange notion that Indian depredations might thereby be avoided, a site for the projected institution was actually purchased on an obscure island in the Susquehanna River. The ambitious Maecenas also outlined a curriculum for his *academia* that included instruction in the fine arts. But the anticipated failure of heirs reckoned without the fertility of Palmer's line, so *Academia Virginiensis et Oxoniensis* collapsed within the framework of his will.

Virginians eventually concluded that a seat of higher learning could best be secured through their own efforts. During the first half of the seventeenth century impetus had been mainly supplied by various pious, philanthropic, and evangelical individuals in England. During the latter half of the century the movement began to draw support from the settlers themselves.

That this favorable attitude on their part failed to develop earlier can be ascribed to several factors.[15] In the first place, the planters possessed insufficient means to underwrite such costly ventures. Great wealth concentrated in the hands of an enlightened segment of the colonial population materialized only in the latter part of the century. A large percentage of the earlier colonists, moreover, regarded England as home: Virginia was merely a fabled El Dorado in which financial betterment could be sought. These hopeful transients entertained little concern for the intellectual or cultural requirements of the colony and thus lent no support to any efforts aimed at creating a provincial seat of higher learning. Others who had become more firmly rooted were anxious to achieve a pattern of life that had fired their aspirations in England. A vital aspect of the tradition they hoped to perpetuate was an English university education for their sons. Many a tender youth was dispatched on a perilous Atlantic voyage to uphold this genteel pretension.

The colony, as a matter of fact, was still in a frontier status, its population sparse and widely dispersed. The census of 1635 listed fewer than 5,000 inhabitants; in 1649 the number had risen only to 15,000.[16] Related to this was an agricultural economy that discouraged the growth of cities and towns. Had urban centers developed, educational ventures would doubtless have received earlier and more active provincial support.

The colonial government itself showed scant official interest in the problem. Office was regarded mainly as a means for personal advancement. The Virginia Company, especially under the farsighted leadership of Sir Edwin Sandys, had pursued a liberal and enlightened policy in colonial administration. But the reactionary disposition of the Stuarts was frequently reflected in the policies pursued by their Virginia appointees after the colony became a royal province in 1624. The fact that royal support and backing for a college obtained only after the Glorious Revolution of 1688 is significant.

By the middle of the century other influences began to counteract these retarding factors. The population of the colony rose to a substantial 40,000 persons in 1666.[17] English university graduates among the planters and within the professional classes increased, strengthening public sentiment in favor of the establishment of schools and colleges. A failure to attract an adequate supply of clergymen from England disturbed the pious, who began to direct their attention toward the possibility of founding a provincial seminary for training ministers of the gospel. Great wealth began to accumulate in the hands of the planter class, producing an aristocracy of greater and lesser landowners whose ideal was rapidly becoming a colonial modification of the English aristocratic tradition. And the dangers and perils of the voyage abroad began to stir the compassion of parents formerly bent on educating their heirs in English schools and colleges.

Private libraries of considerable size, moreover, were beginning to take shape. These collections were being assembled not only by members of the planter aristocracy but also by representatives of the middle class.[18] Their interest in books was indicative of a concern for higher education and for intellectual ideals. To be sure, a growing pride in Virginia also began to permeate the colonial mind.

In 1660 the Virginia General Assembly gave expression to these underlying sentiments by passing at least three different acts aimed at establishing a public free school and college. One of the measures provided

for the advance of learning, education of youth, supply of the ministry, and promotion of piety, [that] there be land taken upon purchases for a Colledge and free schoole, and that there be, with as much speed as may be convenient, housing erected thereon for entertainment of students and schollers.[19]

Another statute referred to the projected institution as "a college of students of the liberal arts."[20]

It was proposed that the requisite funds be raised through personal subscriptions on the part of the colonists. Such a subscription was made. Despite his despotic disposition, Governor Sir William Berkeley, together with the members of his Council, contributed to the project. The justices of the county courts, the next wealthiest group in the colony, were urged to follow suit. And a memorial, submitted to Berkeley, suggested that the king be petitioned for letters patent authorizing collections from "well-disposed people in England."[21]

But the promised subscriptions were difficult to collect, plantations and settlements remained widely scattered, and, indeed, the public mind was diverted from college plans by the discord and poverty that culminated in 1676 in Bacon's Rebellion. Financial backing, as a matter of fact, was not forthcoming until 1688–89, when "a Small Remnant of Men of Better Spirit, who had either had the benefit of better Education themselves in their Mother-Country, or at least had heard of it from others," subscribed £2,500 to endow an institution of higher learning.[22] This encouragement enabled the active promoters of the venture to proceed with the undertaking. James Blair, commissary of the bishop of London, and Francis Nicholson, lieutenant-governor of the colony, were the principal movers.

Blair, born in Scotland in 1655, was a product of Marischal College, Aberdeen, an institution endowed, it might be noted, with a chair of divinity that had been established by Rev. Patrick Copeland of East India School memory.[23] Blair also held a master of arts degree from the University of Edinburgh. Fortified with Anglican orders, he removed to England, where, from 1682 to 1685, he was employed in the office of the master of rolls at London. While in London he became acquainted with the bishop of the diocese, Henry Compton, who persuaded him to go to Virginia as a missionary. Blair reached the colony in 1685 and assumed the living of Varina parish. Varina parish, significantly enough, embraced the site of the 1617–22 abortive attempt to establish a university and college at Henrico.

Evidences of the ill-fated venture may have survived in the locality, reproachful reminders of miscarried plans and thwarted hopes. Blair's outstanding abilities led in 1689 to his appointment as commissary, or deputy, to the bishop of London, whose episcopal jurisdiction extended to Virginia. Blair, in his new capacity, inaugurated the policy of holding occasional convocations of the Virginia clergy. In 1690, at the first of these conventions, he urged the clergy to take the initiative in founding a free school and college.

The same year that marked the appointment of Blair as commissary also saw the arrival in Virginia of Colonel Francis Nicholson, newly appointed lieutenant-governor of the colony.[24] Nicholson, a professional colonial administrator, had previously served as lieutenant-governor of the short-lived Dominion of New England. Like Blair, he was a man of determined character and sanguine temperament. In 1690, during the absence of Governor Lord Howard of Effingham, Nicholson proposed to the Virginia Council that the "design of a free school and college," already projected by some "pious men," be revived and urged that subscriptions be solicited for its support.[25] The Council, pleased with the proposal, called upon the county justices to submit returns listing the names of planters within their respective localities who might assist the project. The response was heartening.

In consequence, the House of Burgesses in May 1691 directed Blair to proceed to England for the purpose of submitting a memorial to the king and queen, William and Mary, on behalf of the projected establishment.

The mission was in capable hands. Blair reached London

on September 1, 1691, and promptly sought the advice
and assistance of the Anglican hierarchy. Bishop Compton, on whose shoulders rested the burden of Virginia's
spiritual needs, displayed great interest; other prelates—
Stillingfleet, bishop of Worcester; Burnet, bishop of Salis-
bury; Tillotson, archbishop of Canterbury—were equally
enthusiastic.[26] The influence of these powerful church-
men, combined with the liberal disposition of the newly
installed royal authorities, paved the way for Blair's
success.

On November 12, 1691, under the auspices of an introduction by Archbishop Tillotson, Blair laid his memorial
before William III. Graciously received, the memorial was
referred to the proper officials for further consideration.
Two years elapsed, however, while it wended its way
through the intricacies of Whitehall's administrative maze.
Finally, on February 8, 1693, a royal charter authorizing a
college in Virginia was placed in the supplicant's hands.
Blair was designated its first president "during his natural
life," and the institution, the second seat of higher learning
founded in British North America, was "called and de-
nominated, for ever, the College of William and Mary, in
Virginia."[27] The charter specified that the college was authorized in order that "the Church of Virginia may be
furnished with a Seminary of Ministers of the Gospel, and
that the Youth may be piously educated in good Letters
and Manners, and that the Christian Faith may be propa-
gated amongst the Western Indians."[28]

While awaiting the outcome of his mission, Blair, a
practical man, devoted considerable time to the problem of
securing financial support for the proposed seat of learn-

ing. Through the good offices of Bishop Burnet a sizable segment of a bequest left by Hon. Robert Boyle for "charitable and pious uses" was obtained.[29] That sum, earmarked for the education of Indians, was subsequently invested in Brafferton Manor, Yorkshire; it furnished the college with regular revenues until the American revolution. Blair also secured the passage of an order-in-council enabling certain former pirates to regain portions of their seized property by contributing £300 to the college coffers.[30] The king and queen confirmed their benevolence by subscribing £2,000 out of the Virginia quitrents toward the erection of the necessary academic buildings.[31] Their government made an exceedingly handsome settlement by levying a tax for the support of the college of one penny on every pound of tobacco exported from Virginia and Maryland and by granting the college all profits and fees deriving from the office of the Virginia surveyor-general.[32] The college was even more closely allied to the colonial economy when the Virginia General Assembly in 1693 levied for its maintenance a permanent export duty on skins and furs.[33] These financial arrangements integrated the destiny of the college with that of the colony. Virginia on the threshold of her golden age offered brilliant prospects indeed.

Blair, during his English sojourn, also occupied himself with the development of plans for the administration, organization, and curriculum of the projected seat of learning. Problems touching these points were discussed frequently in letters directed to Colonel Nicholson.[34] Blair was conscious, for example, of "the vast difference there is between the contrivance of our Virginia college & all the

Colleges I can hear of here in England."[35] To be sure, he and his associates did not slavishly strive to model the Virginia institution on the pattern of its English counterparts. A realistic appreciation of colonial needs led at the outset to modifications of English university practice and precedent. Blair distrusted in particular the lecture system employed in English universities. Professors in the Virginia college, he decided, "must daily examine their Scholars, prescribe them tasks, hear them dispute, try them in all manner of exercises & wait upon them as punctually as a School Mast^r."[36]

Blair envisioned and in the due course of time organized a college having three grades of instruction. The first grade was to consist of a grammar school, where Latin and Greek would be taught. The second was to consist of two schools, one of moral philosophy, the other of natural philosophy and mathematics. The third, designed to qualify young men for the church, was to consist of a school of divinity and a school of oriental languages.[37] In general, a youth was expected to complete his grammar school work at the age of sixteen and then be examined by the college president and masters. If he survived that ordeal, he could be admitted to one of the two philosophical schools. In the school of natural philosophy he could turn to rhetoric, logic, ethics, and natural and civil law. Four years were to be required for a bachelor's degree and seven for a master of arts. If he elected the ministry for a career, the student might enter either of the two divinity schools: one for the study of Hebrew and the Bible, the other for investigating "the common Places of Divinity, and the Controversies with Hereticks."[38]

The power to establish and maintain this "Place of universal study, or perpetual College for Divinity, Philosophy, Languages, and other good Arts and Sciences" was entrusted to a self-perpetuating board of trustees, or visitors, all resident in the colony.[39] The trustees or visitors were authorized annually to elect from their number a rector for the college and every seven years to choose some "eminent and discreet person" as chancellor.[40] Blair, named president in the charter, was, in the same instrument, designated rector. Henry Compton, bishop of London, agreed to serve as the first chancellor. After somewhat heated debate, the trustees decided on Middle Plantation, a small settlement some six miles from the colonial capital at Jamestown, as a site for the institution.[41] Middle Plantation was shortly thereafter renamed Williamsburg in honor of William III. Thus organized, the college authorities turned their attention to plans for erecting a building and for securing the appurtenances essential to a seat of higher learning.

CHAPTER TWO

The First Book Collection
1693–1705

JAMES BLAIR, shortly after arriving in London in 1691 on his mission to secure a charter for the college, wrote to Francis Nicholson in Virginia urging agreement on the early appointment of a president for the projected seat of learning. One of Blair's arguments in favor of the move stressed the need for "overseeing of the . . . Library."[1] Such concern perhaps indicates that Blair sought to collect books for the projected library during the course of his two-year stay in England. Many of the dignitaries whose patronage was solicited—John Tillotson, Gilbert Burnet, Anthony Horneck, Henry Compton, Edward Stillingfleet—were distinguished men of letters. It is unlikely that a man as enterprising as Blair would have failed to mention the desirability of including the printed works of those eminent divines in the college collection. That form of flattery, as a matter of fact, would have been a means of ingratiating himself, as well as the college project, into their favor and esteem. It is also reasonable to assume that Blair made efforts to obtain the printed works of Robert Boyle, whose eleemosynary bequest helped finance the academic venture. Blair negotiated the Boyle transaction with the philosopher's nephew, Richard Boyle, first earl of Burlington.[2] Because Blair resorted principally to personal interviews in seeking support for the project, he left sparse documentation of his activities. This complicates the problem of determining whether he made efforts to acquire books and, if so, whether his efforts met with success. The detailed expense accounts that Blair kept for the mission fail to show that he returned to Virginia in 1693 with crates of books.[3] This, of course, is not conclusive proof that none were obtained, for the transportation of such materials would have been handled by the college's London agent, Micajah Perry.[4]

Additional evidence that the founders contemplated library needs even before the college was formally organized can be seen in the terms of the charter. It specifically enjoined the trustees to employ the initial funds "only for defraying the Charges that shall be laid out in Erecting and Fitting the Edifices of the said intended College, and furnishing them with books and other utensils."[5] The declaration of academic aims set forth in the preamble to the charter would presumably have governed the formulation of plans for the organized acquisition of library materials. But more likely than not plans of this nature existed only in the mind of President Blair. Upon returning to Virginia in 1693, he assumed active control of the project.

Both Blair and his principal assistant, Headmaster Mungo Ingles of the grammar school, held degrees as masters of arts from Edinburgh. Recollections of Edinburgh may have come to mind when the two set about forming a library for William and Mary. Neither Blair nor any of his colleagues in the undertaking were well acquainted with

1.   James Blair (1655–1743), first president of the College of William and Mary. From a portrait attributed to Charles Bridges. The east front of the college, as reconstructed after the fire of 1705, is shown in the background, rising above the legendary phoenix. (Courtesy of College of William and Mary)

2. East front of the College of William and Mary in 1702. From a drawing by Franz Ludwig Michel. (Courtesy of College of William and Mary)

Harvard College in New England, which then supported the only other college library in the colonies.

The Edinburgh library, as recalled by Blair and Ingles, served merely as a reading room.[6] Its volumes did not circulate and, indeed, many were still firmly attached to the bookcases by medieval chains. Not until 1688 was a visitor able to commend Edinburgh's librarian for having bookcases enclosed with wire. Strict regulations were in effect, moreover, to prevent damage to and destruction of the books. William Henderson, "who showed great zeal and fidelity in his office," was Edinburgh's librarian during Blair's student days. And Henderson's son, Robert, who achieved distinction by introducing *bibliothekswissen-schaft* into the management of the Edinburgh library, held the post when Ingles was in residence.

Blair was also able to recall—not from firsthand experience, perhaps, for undergraduate use of college libraries was a much later development—the library of Marischal College, Aberdeen, where he had secured his bachelor's degree. It is doubtful that his three years' experience in the office of the master of rolls at London served any useful purpose in setting up the William and Mary collection of printed books.

Library plans could not be pursued aggressively at William and Mary until suitable accommodations were available for housing books. The main college building, "adapted to the Nature of the Country" from drawings attributed to Sir Christopher Wren, Surveyor-General of the King's Works, was begun in 1694 and was first occupied in 1697.[7] It was the most ambitious collegiate edifice erected during the colonial period of American history. It is certain that the plans included accommodations for the library. Since 1380, when William of Wykeham founded New College, Oxford, the plans for every English college had provided space for an institutional book collection.[8]

Wren, who is credited with the plans for the first building at William and Mary, was keenly interested in library planning. His work on the Lincoln Cathedral library in 1674, his celebrated design in 1676 for the New Library at Trinity College, Cambridge, and his St. Paul's Cathedral library at London, all antedated the drafting of plans for the collegiate structure in Virginia.[9] Wren, moreover, greatly influenced his successors in library planning, for though he did not actually introduce the wall system of shelf arrangement into England, he developed and successfully adapted it to English requirements.

The long front or façade of the William and Mary structure faced due east, and virtually all of its major rooms, with the exception of the great hall and the chapel, which respectively were to form the north and south links of a projected quadrangle, enjoyed eastern exposures. This orientation enabled the builders, consciously or unconsciously, to follow the precept of Vitruvius that "libraries ought to have an eastern exposure because their purposes require the morning light and also because books in such libraries will not decay."[10] The precise location of the library room in the original structure is not revealed in the surviving records. But the most likely location would have been on the second floor.

The spacious basements and cellars of the building were given over to kitchens, storerooms, pantries, butteries, and other housekeeping arrangements. On the main floor were quarters for the grammar school, rooms for advanced classes, a great hall, a wide covered piazza, and, after 1732, the chapel.[11] The second floor provided space for an impressive chamber—designated the "Blue Room"—in which the president and masters, as well as the board of visitors, could transact their official business, as well as more classrooms and living accommodations for students and masters. Additional living quarters for the students and masters were located on the third floor and in the attics.

The notion that a seat of higher learning ought to devote its own funds to acquiring library materials was virtually unknown in the seventeenth century. Professor Morison reports that his examination of English college records for the period 1595–1640 failed to uncover a single instance of a college spending money on books.[12] It was generally believed that a college or university library could be developed solely on the basis of donations and bequests. This belief was given credence in the colonies by the fact that the library cart often preceded the college horse. At Yale, for example, each member of the body of ministers who met in 1700 to consider the advisability of an institution of higher learning for Connecticut agreed to give "books for the founding of a college."[13] The very name of Harvard College, moreover, perpetuates the generosity of a library benefactor. Thus, despite the authorization contained in their charter, little evidence survives to show that the officials at William and Mary earmarked any significant portion of their initial endowments for the development of a library. The magnificent building under construction from 1694 to 1699 absorbed all the available funds.

Indeed, it is not surprising to discover that the first reference to library resources at the college occurs in connection with a donation. Francis Nicholson, "the Great Maecenas of the College," heads the list of known library benefactors. A catalogue of his private library, endorsed May 30, 1695, and now preserved in the Fulham Palace archives, is prefaced by a statement that Nicholson wished to leave the entire collection to William and Mary.[14] His generous disposition preceded the preparation of the catalogue, for contemporary annotations indicate that seven volumes from the collection had already been turned over to the college. The titles so marked were Robert South's *Animadversion upon Dr. Sherlock's book entitled A vindication of the holy and ever-blessed Trinity;* three works of Gilbert Burnet, *A discourse of the pastoral care, The life of William Bedell,* and *The life and death of Sir Matthew Hale;* an anonymous work entitled *The art of catechising: or, The compleat catechist;* Burnet's translation of Sir Thomas More's *Utopia;* and, appropriately enough, John Locke's enlightened *Some thoughts concerning education.* No earlier evidence than the record of these accessions, received before May 30, 1695, remains to show that books were actually being assembled for the library.

The college did not have to wait for Nicholson's demise in order to obtain the rest of his books. They apparently were donated to the library when Nicholson returned to Virginia in 1698 to reassume the reins of government. This may have led the Virginia House of Burgesses to affirm the following year that, after the king, Nicholson was "the most zealous patron of the New Seat of Learning."[15] Nicholson retained in his possession a copy of the catalogue receipted by College Clerk William Robertson. It was subsequently employed when he sought to vindicate the eccentric personal behavior that characterized his conduct during his second sojourn in the colony, 1698–1705.[16] The vindication, published in 1727, contained a rueful estimate that the books presented to the college cost a good fifty or sixty pounds sterling.[17]

The Nicholson catalogue covers a collection of well over two hundred volumes.[18] Of this number, 158 works were specifically listed by title. These titles are grouped according to the sizes of the respective volumes under three headings, (1) folios, (2) quartos, and (3) octavos and duodecimos. Valuations are supplied in most cases, affording a check on Nicholson's 1727 estimate of the total value of the collection. Positive identification of the listed works is occasionally complicated by the free rendition of a title or else by complete absence or incorrect spelling of an author's name. One entry under the quartos covers "thirty-nine books and pamphlets relating to the several sorts of trade and commerce." This is the only entry matching that favorite yet frustrating colonial cataloguing phrase, "a parcel of old books." Even here the cataloguer was thoughtful enough to indicate the subject nature of the volumes so lightly dismissed. A large percentage of the works were printed after 1690, which suggests that Nicholson formed the collection between 1692 and 1694 while in England awaiting a new colonial assignment. The donation provided a nucleus or core around which a library could be developed, and possibly served the useful purpose of encouraging other friends of the college to follow Nicholson's example.

The library thus accessioned a collection that was mainly theological in nature. Its Protestant tone failed to substantiate, moreover, the implications of rumors that the donor had once kneeled during Mass said in the tent of James II on Hounslow Heath.[19] The Biblical commentaries, catechistical and inspirational works, and studies touching dogma, doctrine, and ecclesiastical history were appropriate to the library of an institution dedicated to the propagation of the Anglican faith. The subject matter of the thirty-five folios provides a key to the entire collection. These heavy volumes included copies of Richard Hooker's *Of the lawes of ecclesiastical politie*, Gabriel Towerson's *Explication of the decalogue* and *Explication of the Lord's prayer*, John Strype's inspiring *Memorials of . . . Thomas Cranmer*, the works of Henry Hammond and of Joseph Mede, the sermons of Edward Stillingfleet, Hugh Davis' *De jvre vniformitatis ecclesiasticae*, and William Cave's historical study *Antiquitates apostolicae*. The octavos included, naturally enough, a copy of *The works of the learned and pious author of The whole duty of man*.

Devotional works comprised a large segment of the collection. John Kettlewell's widely read *Measures of Christian obedience* was present; so were copies of Sir Matthew Hale's *Contemplations moral and divine*, Robert Boyle's *Seraphic love*, Abraham Seller's *Devout communicant*, and John Tillotson's *Rule of faith*. Ecclesiastical history was represented by Louis Ellies Dupin's *Evangelical history;* William Cave's *Primitive Christianity* and *Dissertation concerning the government of the ancient church,* the latter describing "the rise and growth of the First Church of God"; John Sleidan's important *General history of the reformation;* and Peter, Lord King's *Enquiry into the constitution, discipline, unity and worship of the primitive church.*

Factional dispute, which engaged many learned seventeenth-century minds, was represented by such works as Robert South's previously mentioned *Animadversion upon Dr. Sherlock's book* and by copies of Samuel Clarke's *Demonstration of the divine authority of the law of nature,* Thomas Roger's *True Protestant bridle,* and William Sherlock's *Vindication of the doctrine of the holy and ever blessed Trinity.* Polemics accounted for numerous anti-Quaker tracts. These included John Faldo's *Quakerism no Christianity,* Henry Hallywell's *Account of familism as revived by the Quakers,* William Allen's bitter little volume entitled *Grand errour of the Quakers detected,* and John Norris' *Two treatises concerning the divine light.*

Other polemical works calculated to edify Protestant thought appeared on the college shelves as a result of Nicholson's piety and generosity. Edward Fowler's *Examinations of Cardinal Bellarmine's fourth note of the church* was present; so were copies of Edward Stillingfleet's *Discourse concerning the idolatry practised in the Church of Rome,* Edward Gee's *Jesuit's memorial,* and the more scholarly *Letters of Father Paul,* a production of the celebrated Venetian friar, Paolo Sarpi. One of the more curious diatribes among these treatises was directed by John

Williams at the strange sect discussed in his *Absurd and mischievous principles of the Muggletonians considered.*

The usual assemblage of sermons popular with colonial readers could be found in the Nicholson donation. Wilkins, Glanvill, Hezekiah Burton, Tillotson, Stillingfleet, Clagett, Wake, and Burnet were well represented. And among the miscellaneous religious works were copies of D'Emiliane's *Short history of monastical orders*, John Conrad Werndly's Calvinistic *Liturgia Tigurina*, Bishop Jewel's *Apology*, Symon Patrick's *Mensa mystica*, as well as innumerable "paraphrases."

Aside from a formidable array of Anglican learning and devotion, the Nicholson collection failed to emphasize any particular field of literary interest. Belles-lettres made a scattered showing in such works as Samuel Wesley's heroic poem entitled *The life of Our Blessed Lord and Saviour Jesus Christ*, in the prose and poetry of Abraham Cowley, and in the essays of Montaigne, Saint-Évremond, and Sir William Temple.

History, travel, and biography were more generously treated. Heading the list was Sir Walter Raleigh's *Historie of the world*, a work greatly admired in seventeenth-century Virginia. The presence of a copy of Raleigh's *Remains* was an additional token of the author's popularity. The popularity of another great figure in Virginia history was demonstrated by the presence of two historical studies treating the reign of Queen Elizabeth, Camden's *History of . . . Princess Elizabeth* and Edmund Bohun's *Character of Queen Elizabeth*. Nicholson's donation also brought to the library copies of Christopher Helwich's *Historical and chronological theatre*, Edward D'Auvergne's *History of the last campagne in the Spanish Netherlands*, George

Walter Story's finely illustrated *Impartial history of the wars of Ireland*, and an anonymous work entitled *An historical account of the memorable actions of the most glorious monarch, William III.*

Among the notable pieces of Americana in the accession were copies of Increase Mather's *Brief history of the vvarr with the Indians*, George Warren's *Impartial description of Surinam*, Acosta's *Natural and moral history of the East and West Indies*, Thomas Gage's *New survey of the West Indies*, and the anonymously produced *Relation of the invasion and conquest of Florida by the Spaniards*. Travel and description were further buttressed by copies of Lewis Du May's *Estate of the empire . . . of Germany*, Gabriel de Megalhaen's *New history of the empire of China*, an account of the earl of Carlisle's Russian mission by Guy Miege entitled *Relation of three embassies*, and Jean de Thévenot's *Travels . . . into the Levant*. Useful adjuncts to these relations were present in the form of Edmund Bohun's *Geographical dictionary* and Robert Morden's *Geography rectified.*

Nicholson's gift failed to supply much sustenance in the classics. Here could be noted copies of Sir Robert Stapylton's translation of Pliny's *Panegyricke*, Meric Casaubon's translation of Marcus Aurelius Antonius' *Meditations*, John Norris' translation of *Hierocles upon the golden verses of the Pythagoreans*, and an abridgment of Caesar's *Commentaries*, but not a single volume in the original tongue.

Nicholson, however, was conscious of Whitehall's goals for its colonial appointees, for his books exhibited considerable strength in materials relating to trade and commerce. This brought to the library copies of Gerard de

Malynes' widely quoted *Lex mercatoria*, Lewis Roberts' useful *Merchants mappe of commerce*, Sir Josiah Child's important *Discourse about trade*, and Roger Coke's *England's improvements*. These volumes were backed up by copies of John Smith's *England's improvement reviv'd*, William Leybourn's *Panarithmologia*, Thomas Mun's *England's treasure by forraign trade*, Thomas Houghton's work on American and African gold and silver mining entitled *Royal institutions*, and the thirty-nine unspecified books and pamphlets on trade and commerce in general.

The books on gardening and husbandry that the library received from Nicholson may have been inappropriate to the college collection. In any event, the donation included copies of Jean de La Quintinie's *Compleat gard'ner*, Evelyn's famous *Sylva* and the separate edition of his *Kalendarium Hortense*, Leonard Meager's *English gardener*, John Worlidge's practical *Systema agriculturae*, John Pechey's *Compleat herbal*, and Moses Cooke's *Manner of raising, ordering and improving forest-trees*. Related to these, but perhaps of greater academic value, was a copy of Sir Thomas Pope Blount's *Natural history*.

The rest of the books in the donation touched diverse subjects. Several courtesy books, books that a seventeenth-century Virginia gentleman's library was sure to contain, were present. Among these were editions of Nicholas Cox's *Gentleman's recreation*, and Baltasar Gracian's *Courtier's oracle*. More welcome, perhaps, to the college shelves were Nicholson's copies of Elisha Coles's *English dictionary*, William Evats' translation of Grotius' *Rights of war and peace*, George Tully's *Discourse of the government of the thoughts*, and Milton's *Letters of state*.

The first disbursement of college funds on behalf of the library was made in 1697. Building accounts forwarded to England that year by Governor Sir Edmond Andros carried an entry dated February 27 for the disbursement of £32/11/10 for "books Mapps & papers as per Accot."[20] No other details regarding this sizable expenditure were supplied. The same accounts, however, carry another entry covering the purchase of "Bloomes History of the Bible," that is, Nicholas Fontaine's *History of the Old Testament* and *History of the New Testament* issued by the enterprising publisher, Richard Blome.[21] The funds for this purchase, in the amount of £1/10/—, were given by a friendly London merchant, Sir Jeffrey Jeffreys. The second major expenditure—to be sure, the only other major expenditure that can be dredged from the surviving records of the original library—was made possible with funds contributed by "Dr. Bray's Associates." A donation of £50 for the acquisition of library books was received from that philanthropic source prior to 1700.[22] But again no records remain to show what was acquired. Contributions from the "Associates" might have become more frequent had not considerable coolness developed between Bray and the cantankerous Blair.[23]

Donations of books from English friends of the college began to reach Williamsburg before the century ended. This was publicly noted in a 1699 May Day speech by one of the "scholars," whose eloquence bore the imprint of Blair's adroit coaching:

and here I must not omitt the generosity of the two famous Bishops of London & Sarum, who has broke the Ice to the other Bishops, in making a noble present of well chosen bookes to our Library, intending hereby to take care that our Youth be well seasoned with the best principles of Religion and Learning that can be taught by the most sound & Orthodox Divines.[24]

The ice was broke indeed, but the titles of the "well chosen" books donated by Bishops Compton and Burnet were left to conjecture. Mungo Ingles asserted some years later that the resources of the original library had come mainly as gifts from the bishop of London. But this officious observation must be discounted inasmuch as it is set forth in a petition which the canny Scot addressed to Bishop Compton begging books on his own behalf.[25] The natural patron of the library was the bishop of London. It lay within his ecclesiastical jurisdiction and, as a general rule, he alternated with the archbishop of Canterbury as its chancellor. Throughout the colonial period, moreover, the president of the college served as the bishop's commissary or personal representative in Virginia.

The same "scholar" who praised Bishops Compton and Burnet for their generosity, optimistically added:

This example will be quickly followed by the present Lord Primate of England, a worthy successor to Dr. Tillotson, who continues to water this Nursery wch his predecessor took such pains to plant.[26]

Dr. Tenison, the prelate in question, was not moved by this expression of confidence to emulate his spiritual associates. And had not Blair taken steps to correct any misapprehensions existing in his Grace's mind, the "Nursery" might have waited in vain for nourishment from Lambeth. Blair reminded the archbishop of his derelictions, claiming: "I must continue to beg, that if it lies in your Grace's way you will encourage our new City of Williamsburg, and help our College Library."[27]

The plea was shortly joined by a more positive supplication, dated May 29, 1700, in which Blair informed Tenison that

I must upon this occasion beg leave to put your Grace in mind of your good intentions to help our Library to some good books. We are of opinion that if application were made to the severall good authors in England, they would enrich it at least with a present of their own books. And the Governours of our College have desired me to signify this much to your Grace that if you will employ any young Scholar that you think fit to ask books for us, we will allow him 20 pound a year for his pains. I have enclosed a Catalogue of what Books we have at present that your Grace may the better judge what we want. If any books are procured, let them be sent to the house of Mr. Micajah Perry a Virginia merchant in Leaden hall Street over against the end of Billiter Lane, who will take care to send them to us, and will likewise pay the charges of packing &c., and the said 20 pound.[28]

How far these enterprising efforts were rewarded cannot be fully ascertained. Yet the archbishop notified Nicholson in 1701 that "I have some books for Yor Library but have not sent them yet. . . . Nevertheless what is delayed is not designed not to be performed."[29] The catalogue mentioned in Blair's letter, which would constitute an invaluable addition to the records of the first book collection formed by the college, has either been destroyed or misplaced.

In this respect, it can be noted that Thomas Hearne,

antiquarian and Bodleian library keeper, recorded in his journal shortly after the first book collection at William and Mary was destroyed by fire that

letters from Virginia say that the College at Williamsburg, a most Stately Fabrik & one of the best in all America, & to wch the late King Wm had been a Benefactor, was on the 29th of October last [1705] utterly consum'd by fire wch by an unknown accident broke out in the very dead of the Night together with the Library, to wch divers persons bearing any Love to Learning had been Contributors, & in all probability would in some time have grown very famous.[30]

This observation came from a professional librarian, familiar with the intricacies of his calling and well acquainted among the English literati of his day. His comments on the "divers persons" who contributed to the library would seem to indicate a knowledge of the aforementioned efforts to solicit books from "the severall good authors" in England.

Such diligence in seeking contributions for the library in England should not be construed as an indication that opportunities in Virginia were neglected. Some of the more active colonial promoters of the college possessed plantation libraries of considerable size and distinction. Three of the six private book collections analyzed by Louis B. Wright in his *First gentlemen of Virginia* were owned by members of the college board of visitors—Ralph Wormeley II, Robert ("King") Carter, and William Byrd II. In the search for benefactors, these collectors would have been fair targets. The Philip Ludwells—the elder brother-in-law to James Blair and the younger soon to become a member of the board of visitors—may have donated books from the library at Green Spring, the Lud-well seat near Williamsburg. It is idle but intriguing to speculate on the works that could have come from such a source. The Green Spring collection was begun by Sir William Berkeley, a man of literary pretensions and the author of several dramatic pieces.[31]

Even visitors passing through Virginia were approached in the campaign to secure books for the library. The only volume known to have survived the fire of 1705, a copy of Paolo Sarpi's *History of the Council of Trent*, was the gift of an English sea captain who occasionally made the Virginian voyage. This volume, recovered by the college in 1947, carries an inscription stating that it was "The Gift of Captain Nicholas Humfrys, Commander of the Ship Hart-well to Wm & Mary College, Anno 1703/4."[32]

But the college remained little more than a grammar school for nearly two decades following its establishment. The actual need for library resources was therefore not acutely felt until early in the eighteenth century. This may explain a failure to uncover any rules governing the administration and use of the original collections. Comments by Hugh Jones in 1724 indicate quite clearly that use of the library was restricted to the college masters.[33] Such a policy would have been in accord with contemporary practice at other collegiate establishments.[34] There is nothing to indicate, though, that any of the books at William and Mary were chained to their cases, despite the fact that English colleges retained the practice until the end of the eighteenth century.[35] The University of Edinburgh, on the other hand, got rid of its chains before 1688,[36] and chains were never used on the library books at William and Mary's colonial counterpart, Harvard in New England.[37]

Hugh Jones's comments also reveal that one of the grammar school ushers was usually charged with the custody of the library "in order to make his Place more agreeable to his merit."[38] As the college was without an usher until 1699, either Blair himself or Mungo Ingles may have filled the post during the interim. This could account in part for the lamentations of the latter, who, in referring to ushers, complained that the first "Dyed at Cowes & he that was to succeed him Marryed a Wife . . . & could not come."[39] William Robertson, who became clerk of the college at the turn of the century, signed a receipt on at least one occasion for books given to the collection.[40] This might mean that his predecessor in the clerkship, Francis Clements, rather than Blair or Ingles, served as first keeper of the library. In fact, if Blair assigned the responsibility to Clements, he could well have pointed out a precedent at Edinburgh, where the secretary of the university was charged with the same duties.[41]

The furnishings of the library room probably consisted of wooden presses or cupboards arranged flat against the walls, plus necessary tables and stools. Just how the books were arranged on the shelves will perhaps remain a mystery. In this respect, it might be noted that the second Bodleian catalogue, published in 1620, recommended that library books be arranged according to size: folio, quarto, octavo, and so on.[42] Perhaps the library keeper at William and Mary followed this advice. The printed Harvard catalogue of 1723 certainly demonstrates that the Massachusetts authorities were guided by the Bodleian precepts.[43]

3. Francis Nicholson (1655–1728), "the Great Maecenas of the College."
From a painting by Alexis Simon Belle. (Courtesy of Virginia Historical
Society)

4. Henry Compton (1632–1713), bishop of London and first chancellor of the College of William and Mary. From an engraving by Isaac Becket based on the portrait by John Riley. (Courtesy of Virginia Historical Society)

The original book collection at William and Mary was not large enough to have presented any problems in classification, so press and shelf marks probably were not used.

Because of the lack of evidence, the nature of these resources, roughly estimated at fewer than one thousand volumes, cannot be properly evaluated. It would be unjustified to surmise that the traits of the Nicholson donation characterized the other components of the collection. That would overlook the Compton and Burnet gifts of "well chosen Bookes," the Tenison and Dr. Bray's Associates contributions, the books actually purchased with college funds, and gifts doubtless received but not recorded in lasting fashion. It is hardly to be expected that in point of size the collection compared very favorably with the older and by then well-established library at Cambridge, Massachusetts. Yet Professor Morison's evaluation of the seventeenth-century Harvard collection as "lots of theology and a little of everything else" could also doubtless be applied to the first collection at the College of William and Mary.[44]

All the high hopes and good intentions embodied in the library were dashed to the ground on October 29, 1705. About eleven o'clock that evening William Eddings, Blair's overseer, who was chasing some stray horses out of a nearby cornfield, discovered that the college building was on fire.[45] The flames spread rapidly and by dawn the building was a gutted ruin.[46] It does not appear likely that any of the books in the library were saved. Several students —including an inevitable scion of the Randolph clan— were hard pressed even to save themselves.[47] If books were salvaged, subsequent fires in 1859 and 1862 obliterated the traces that remained in the possession of the college. The opportunity for pillage was doubtless inviting, so it might be expected that the eye of some unscrupulous bibliophile could well have alighted on a desirable piece. But the previously mentioned copy of Sarpi's *History of the Council of Trent* is the only volume that has turned up to support this possibility.

The loss of books and papers was not confined to the contents of the library room. Benjamin Harrison, Jr., who was residing in the building at the time—or, according to Mungo Ingles, "for his greater Grandeur must needs keep his Court in the Colledge"—lost all of the materials he had collected for a projected history of Virginia.[48] Ingles himself suffered the loss of his "study full of books," which, he declared, cost him "many a deep sigh."[49] These sighs were wafted to Bishop Compton in 1707 when Ingles complained that

I can not enough lament the loss of my books, 18 boxes or shelves crambed as full as could hold, 'tis very much contrary to my Nature to turn beggar, yet willingly be obliged to his Grace my Lord Archbishop of Canterbury, and any of your friends for a small but choice collection of books of Divinity.[50]

One intrepid soul, a Mr. Reedwood, attempted to save a "Genll. Map of the World," presented by Colonel Nicholson, that was hanging in the grammar school room but "durst not for the flame that came pouring in from the south end."[51] The same individual then dashed "out of the School, and saved the Douk of Milan [an otherwise unidentified portrait] that hung next to the dore that opens into the Piazza."[52]

Despite contemporary rumors, there appears to be no reason for believing the fire was other than accidental. Several previous fires, all extinguished in time to avert disaster, were definitely attributed to faulty construction. On this fatal occasion a spark from one of the chimneys found lodgment on the wooden shingles of the roof and from there spread over the entire building. "When I first heard of its being burnt," exclaimed Mungo Ingles, "I had so much charity for all mankind, that I was of opinion that none under a Fury let loose from Hell could be capable of so much Mischief."[53] A less spiritual Virginia General Assembly immediately instituted proceedings to inquire into the calamity, thereby provoking much lively testimony but few definite conclusions.[54]

Several responsible witnesses testified that the fire broke out in the south end of the building and endeavored to imply that it originated in President Blair's chamber chimney. Others argued that the conflagration was the work of three men, ominously "clothed like Gentlemen," who were seen running from the building and across New Kent road shortly after the fire was discovered. In referring to this possibility, an ever-articulate Mungo Ingles offered up the pious hope that "if there be such devils out of Hell, God Almighty will bring their work of darkness to light."[55]

CHAPTER THREE

Rebuilding the Book Collection
1705–1743

A FTER 1705 the college, in the words of Hugh Jones, "revived and improved out of its own Ruins."[1] Reconstruction of the charred edifice got under way with the help of funds contributed by Queen Anne.[2] Governor Alexander Spotswood, another patron of the undertaking, was able to report in 1716 that "the building is well nigh compleated again [and] those under whose Care it is, have resolved to prosecute the original design of its foundation."[3] The college board of visitors, reasonably apprehensive, took appropriate measures to insure the safety of the structure. William Craig, appointed porter in 1716, was given explicit directions to permit no vagrants "to loyter or lodge in the sd Colledge" and to see that "the chimneys be kept clean swept."[4] The visitors also prudently ordered from England "1 ingine for Quenching Fire" and "2 Doz: leather Bucketts with the Colledge Cypher thereon."[5]

The fabric of the building was modified somewhat during the course of its restoration. But there is no reason to believe that the changes, mainly on the exterior, brought about any substantial rearrangement of the interior. A room was definitely set aside for the library.[6] Yet again there are no surviving clues as to its specific location. Notations referring to the assignment of student living quarters later in the century show that it was not on the first floor.[7] And it is not likely that it would have been given space on the third floor, which, in the reconstructed edifice, was reduced on the main front to a half-story lighted by dormer windows. The sloping walls of the modified third-floor rooms would have made them unsuitable for the placement of the presses and cases needed in shelving books. This leaves only the second floor, which is doubtless where the room was located. It can be said with certainty that it did not have northern or southern exposures, for it was flanked by rooms that were occupied as living quarters by students.[8]

The college in 1716 began to acquire academic qualifications that made proper library facilities essential. Two chairs of learning were filled, the one combining philosophy and mathematics going to Rev. Hugh Jones. Jones had performed his undergraduate and graduate work at Jesus College, Oxford, where he had learned what to expect of an institution of higher learning. These ideas, applied to Virginia, were ably expounded in his *Present state of Virginia* published in 1724.

Little had been done to invigorate the library program prior to Jones's arrival. Indeed, the first reference to a library accession after the fire of 1705 occurs in 1716 in connection with the dismissal from the faculty of the unfortunate Arthur Blackamore. President Blair and Mungo Ingles had violently parted company in 1705, at which time Blackamore succeeded Ingles as head of the grammar school. But, alas, Blackamore was more often in his cups than out and finally, in 1716, was placed on probation by

the board of visitors. "If he behaves himselfe well," the
visitors decided, "he [is to] be allowed and paid £12
curr[e]nt money."⁹ But the reward was not high enough.
After one final binge the wretched schoolmaster was sum-
marily dismissed, only to undergo humiliating financial
embarrassment in seeking passage home to England. The
board of visitors generously acquitted Blackamore of sizable debts due the college and ordered that "the Books &
Globes belonging to the said Blackamore be valued and
purchased for the use of the Colledge Library."¹⁰ No re-
ceipts or other records remain to show what the library
acquired through this dispensation. In view of Blackamore's training—he was a graduate of Christ Church, Oxford—it is reasonable to suppose that his books reflected
the classical tradition in which he had been grounded.¹¹

The only surviving proof that English friends of the
college remembered the depleted status of its library resources during the period of reconstruction can be found
in a copy of John Gibbon's *Introductio ad Latinam blasoniam* held by the Library of Congress. A longhand inscription on the flyleaf states:

Ego: Author [*sic*] huius libri, donavi eundem Bibliothecae
Collegij nuper fundati in Virginia. Sic Testor propria mea
manuscriptione aetatis meae 87: 1717.
[signed] Johannes Gibbon.

Gibbon had enjoyed the hospitality of Virginia in 1659
and 1660 as the guest of Colonel Richard Lee. In 1660,
after the restoration of the Stuarts, he returned to England
and devoted the remainder of a long life (1629–1718) to
heraldic pursuits. His *Introductio ad Latinam blasoniam*
contains textual references to his sojourn in Virginia, and

the Library of Congress copy is embellished with manuscript annotations also relating to his stay in the colony. Both the Latin inscription quoted above and the manuscript notes were characteristic of the author. His biographer explains that after Gibbon was promoted to the College of Arms as Bluemantle Pursuivant "he injured himself by his arrogance towards his less learned superiors . . . whose shortcomings he had an unpleasant habit of registering in the margins of library books, which he also filled with calculations of his own nativity."[12] A good Latinist has concluded that the Library of Congress copy "of this book"—*huius libri*—was almost certainly not the copy that Gibbon donated to the college in 1717. Gibbon's use of the word "the same"—*eundem*—in his reference to the gift, the Latinist explains, consequently means no more than a copy of the "same" work.[13]

Hugh Jones was distressed by the inadequacies of the book collection that he found at the college in 1716. Even so, the hopeless picture of the library that he painted in 1724 has familiar undertones of promotional endeavor:

For it is now a College without a Chapel, without a Scholarship, and without a Statute. There is a Library without Books, comparatively speaking, and a President without a fix'd Salary till of Late. . . . These things greatly impede the Progress of Sciences and learned Arts, and discourage those that may be inclined to contribute their Assistance or Bounty towards the Good of the College.[14]

In his more detailed treatment of the library and what ought to be done to improve its condition, Jones admitted it "is better furnished of late than formerly by the kind Gifts of several Gentlemen."[15] Unfortunately, he neglected mentioning the names of the benefactors and did not describe their donations. In assessing the library collections, Jones also observed that "the number of Books is but very small, and the Sets upon each Branch of Learning are very imperfect, and not the best of the Sort." In order to remedy the defect, he recommended steps recalling the earlier efforts made by Blair to solicit books from "the severall good authors in England." Jones suggested that application be made to the societies and superior clergy in England, "who would give at least what Duplicates they have upon such an useful Occasion."

The sets and collections that could not be obtained through gifts should be purchased, Jones stipulated, as soon as the college might find funds for restocking the library. These funds, he believed, would be forthcoming from "the Clergy, Burgesses, and Gentry of the Country, if upon easy Terms they were allowed the Use of the Library at certain Hours, at such Times as they shall be at Williamsburgh, either for Pleasure or upon Business."[16] This enlightened proposal came firmly to grips with the need for modifying traditional concepts of college library functions to the requirements of colonial life. The college library needed financial support, Jones reasoned, and the colonial population needed a public library, so why not satisfy the former by meeting the needs of the latter?

Jones's proposal to open the library to a select constituency of the public is surprising in view of his conservative thoughts respecting collegiate use of the book collection. His recommendations on this score merely reaffirmed a traditional policy of restricting the library facilities to the masters and graduate students:

Such scholars, Commoners, and Servitors, as have behaved themselves well, and minded their Studies for three Years, and can pass proper Examination, and have performed certain Exercises, should have the Degree of a Batchellor of Arts conferred upon them . . . being allowed the Use of the Library as well as the Masters, paying proper Fees upon their Admission for the Good of the Library.[17]

The undergraduate, in other words, did not figure in Jones's scheme for improving the library program. His recommendation for the assessment of library fees supplied a glimpse of things to come, but was not adopted until events fifty years later necessitated that course. Indeed, despite their forceful appeal, no evidence remains to indicate that any of Jones's recommendations got beyond the pages of his book.

Jones's complaints may have influenced the allocation of a bequest of £150 left to the college around 1720 by Colonel Edward Hill of Shirley. The board of visitors, prior to 1729, decided that the full amount would be applied "towards the better furnishing of the Library of the said College with Books."[18] Hill was thereby cast in the role of one of the foremost colonial benefactors of the library. The sum was considerable, but just how it was spent is not reported in the surviving records.

The college in 1727 attained full academic status. All of its chairs were filled with qualified men of learning, and students for the first time were enabled to pursue the full course of instruction envisioned by its founders.[19] On the advice of Chancellor William Wake, archbishop of Canterbury, a set of rules was drawn up for its good government. One of these statutes provided that the library keeper was to be nominated and elected by the president and masters. Perhaps this merely confirmed a longstanding practice. Hugh Jones said that John Harris held the post in 1724.[20] And Harris is the first library keeper whose name is definitely known. His predecessors and his successors down to the middle of the eighteenth century were in all probability, like himself, ushers in the grammar school.

Another clause in the same statutes has denied posterity a glimpse of the detailed regulations under which the library operated:

Because the Circumstances of the College in this its Infancy, will not as yet admit many Officers . . . Therefore referring the Rules concerning the . . . Library-Keeper . . . and other Officers to the President and Masters, who are to direct their Offices and Salaries, as the College shall find them useful and necessary; we shall only at present lay down some Rules concerning the Bursar or College Treasurer.[21]

In 1729 the surviving original trustees of the college, following a schedule established by the 1693 charter, transferred its government and property—"also all the Books to the said College belonging"—to the president and masters.[22] This step, taken on February 27, formally marked the maturity of the foundation. The transfer instrument referred to the fact that the main building "hath in it a convenient Chamber set apart for a Library, besides all other Officers necessary for the said college." An able faculty, recruited from English universities, was nevertheless hampered by the inadequacies of the book collection. In consequence, when the ambitious building program approached completion in 1732, an aggressive campaign was launched to improve the library.

President Blair, whose efforts to develop the book collection had commenced with the founding of the college, led off with a forceful communication to Chancellor Edmund Gibson, bishop of London, explaining:

We are in hopes too, of other bounties towards our library, and perhaps from his Majesty in honor of King William and Queen Mary whose names we bear. My Lord Archbishop of Canterbury did a few years ago signify to us his intentions of a donation towards our Library which we doubt not he will now promote.[23]

William Dawson, a Queens College master of arts who had become professor of moral philosophy at William and Mary in 1729, advanced a more ingenious scheme for securing financial aid.

Dawson, in a letter to Chancellor Gibson dated August 11, 1729, described the recent dedication of the college chapel, the president's house that was being constructed, and the Brafferton building that had been erected for the Indian school in 1723. Following these polite preliminaries, he proceeded to the matter of the library:

In short, my Lord, the whole is only not compleat for want of the most useful and ornamental Furniture, Books. Mr. [John] Randolph, who is intrusted with the negotiations of some public Affairs at Home, will wait on your Lordship and propose a method to supply this Defect in some measure. Now, my Lord, if our humble proposal to lay out part of the Brafferton money which is in Mr. Perry's hands, to this purpose, meets with approbation and encouragement from your Lordship, we have a very convenient room for a Library over the Indian School. My Lord Burlington, I am informed, has promised to present us with the Hon. Mr. Boyle's Picture, which we intend to hang up in the aforesaid Library. His

Philosophical and Theological works, together with those which were written by his encouragement, may be thought no improper part of this Collection. The Books published by our Rt. Rev. Lord and Chancellor would do honour and service to the College. A compleat set of the Classicks is very much wanted.[24]

The Brafferton monies eyed by Dawson were held in trust for the education of Indian youths.[25] The college authorities were therefore obliged to act cautiously in formulating plans for the diversion of those funds to other ends. Richard Boyle, the architect earl of Burlington, justified Dawson's expectations by donating to the college a portrait of Robert Boyle that, miraculously enough, is still hanging in the main building. But no records have survived to show whether Burlington presented books to the library or not.

John Randolph, later knighted for his services to the colony, proceeded on his mission to England, armed with detailed instructions drafted by the president and masters. Randolph was enjoined to remind the chancellor that the college officials were "good husbands" of the Brafferton revenues and that even though a handsome building had been erected for the Indian school, and all the necessary charges defrayed, a balance of some £500 sterling remained in the Brafferton account.[26] Randolph, following these preliminaries, was to stress that "as we do not live in an age of miracles, it is not to be doubted that Indian scholars will want the help of many books to qualify them to become good pastours and teachers." Why not, in other words, lay out part of the £500-Brafferton-fund balance "in a well-chosen library"?

Anticipating the charge that this was merely a subterfuge to enrich the main library, Randolph was instructed to argue that "our funds are so poor, and theirs [that is, the Indians] so rich, that they can better supply us than we them." The college, the memorial continued, provided the Indian school with instructors in "Latine, Greek, and Hebrew, and Philosophy, Mathematics, and Divinity." It was only fair, the president and masters concluded, that "they should in turn help themselves and us to a few necessary books for those studies." To clinch the argument, the president and masters promised that whatever books might be secured by this means would be "reposited in distinct presses marked with the name of Boyle or Brafferton," and that each book would carry an appropriate inscription on its cover. It was further promised that the collection would be housed in the Brafferton building. With the parting shot that "books we think as necessary a means and instrument of their [that is, the Indians'] education, as they paying for their victuals and cloaths," the whole design was left to the discretion of Chancellor Gibson and Lord Burlington, managers of the Boyle bequest.

Randolph was furnished with two catalogues, one listing the books already in the library and the other listing those books that "an ancient minister"—meaning, of course, Rev. James Blair—"designs shortly to leave to it." The authorities thus took suitable precautions to prevent a needless duplication of printed resources in the event Randolph were to succeed in getting his hands on the Brafferton funds. Randolph was directed to take the advice of Chancellor Gibson "concerning the properest books for our use, and their best editions." These maneuvers were successful, producing a letter of credit to Micajah Perry, custodian of the Brafferton funds, authorizing Randolph to draw a sum "not exceeding two hundred and fifty or three hundred pound" for purchasing books.[27]

Randolph was entrusted with other commissions. Supplementary instructions directed him to wait on the archbishop of Canterbury, who "was pleased particularly to signify his good intentions of giving or loaning something towards our Library," and to coordinate his book selecting so as not to duplicate any books that his Grace might give. Randolph was also given carte blanche to treat with any charitable individual who might be interested in the library, "that being at present our chief want."[28]

A regular source of income for the library was tapped when the president and masters petitioned the Virginia General Assembly for financial support. The assembly complied in 1734 by passing "an Act for the Better Support and Encouragement of the College of William and Mary in Virginia." The measure renewed an earlier levy of a duty of one penny on every gallon of rum, brandy, other distilled spirits, and wine imported into the colony and appropriated the sizable sum of £200 per annum therefrom for the use of the college, provided

part thereof shall be laid out and applied for buying such books, for the use of the Scholars and students in the college, as the . . . visitors and governors, or the greater part of them, shall think most necessary; and such books, so to be bought, shall be marked thus, *The Gift of the General Assembly of Virginia in the year 1734*, and shall for ever be preserved and kept in the public library of the said college.[29]

The act was periodically renewed throughout the remaining life of the colonial government.[30] Only one volume purchased with the income from this alcoholic source, a copy of Pitt's translation of *The Aeneid of Virgil*, escaped destruction in the fire of 1859. It still bears on its inner front cover the printed label required by the colonial legislature: *The Gift of the General Assembly of Virginia, in the year 1734.*

Archbishop Wake, of whom much was expected, passed to his reward in 1737. The good man did not forget the anxious Virginians, for his will provided a legacy of fifty pounds for "William & Mary College in Virginia to buy books."[31] President Blair, in whose care the fund was entrusted, turned to Chancellor Gibson for advice as to its proper application. Both agreed "to let the Classicks alone at this time" and to spend the money on "more useful books of Divinity."[32] Gibson himself undertook to make the selections. It cannot be determined what was purchased, but the bishop's choices naturally met with Blair's approval. On May 12, 1739, Gibson was notified that "we have received the late Archbishops donation of Books, and desire to return our most hearty thanks to your Lo[r] for so good a Choice."[33]

Death brought other bequests to the library. Rev. Emanuel Jones, rector of Petsworth parish in Gloucester County, died in 1739, leaving some, if not all, of his books to the college.[34] Only one volume, Arrian's *Enchiridion*, a handbook of Stoic advice by the Greek philosopher Epictetus that Jones had acquired in 1687 while studying at Oriel College, Oxford, somehow or other escaped destruction in the fires of 1859 and 1862. Governor Spotswood, who, despite frequent altercations with the irascible James Blair, cherished friendly feelings for the college, died in 1740, leaving to the library all his "Books, maps and mathematical instruments."[35] Again, only one volume has survived as evidence of the bequest. But this volume must have struck an unusual note in the mighty chorus of theological and philosophical works that lined the library shelves. It is Spotswood's copy of Piganiol de La Force's *Description des châteaux et parcs de Versailles, de Trianon, et de Marly.*

And death in 1743 finally called "the ancient minister" whose firm hand had guided the college and its library for a full half-century. But in death as in life, Blair sought to improve the library. His entire personal collection of books, together with £500 in cash, was left to the college.[36] William Dawson a decade earlier had claimed that Blair did not own "many Good Editions of the Fathers."[37] If patristical literature was wanting, Blair's acquaintance and friendship with scholars in England would certainly have brought to his shelves significant materials on contemporary theological thought. The great monument of sixteenth-century learning, the Antwerp polyglot, described by Blair as "my Arius Montanus' Bible," would have lent distinction to any collection.[38] The catalogue of Blair's library that Sir John Randolph carried to England in 1732 has been lost. And a perusal of Blair's surviving correspondence fails to bring to light supplementary data covering titles in his collection. A nineteenth-century Virginia collector somehow or other acquired a copy of

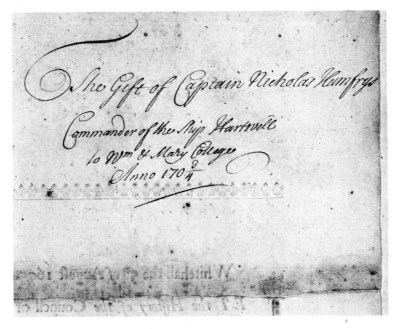

The Gift of Captain Nicholas Humfrys
Commander of the Ship Hartwell
to Wm & Mary College
Anno 170 3/4

5. Presentation inscription in Paolo Sarpi's *History of the Council of Trent*, given to the college in 1703/4 by Captain Nicholas Humfrys. (Courtesy of College of William and Mary)

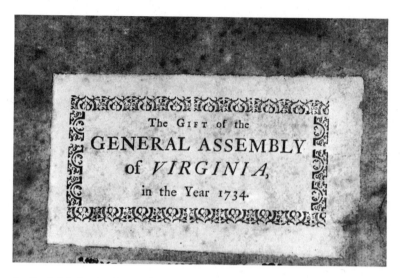

6. Book label affixed to volumes acquired by the College of William and Mary between 1734 and 1776 with funds appropriated from the provincial levy on wines and liquors. (Courtesy of College of William and Mary)

Bryan Robinson's *Treatise of the animal oeconomy* stamped in red with the name of "Doctor James Blair."[39] But all other evidences of the "ancient minister's" legacy to the library were apparently consumed in the fires of 1859 and 1862.

CHAPTER FOUR

Expanding the Book Collection

1743–1776

PRESIDENT BLAIR'S death in 1743 placed the college in the hands of a faculty that was closely allied to Queens College, Oxford. Blair's successor, William Dawson, who had assumed the chair of moral philosophy at William and Mary in 1729, was a veteran of nine years of undergraduate and graduate work at Queens. Dawson, throughout his career in Virginia from 1729 until his death in 1752, maintained close contacts with his former associates at Queens.[1] Dawson's successor as president of the college, William Stith the historian, was also a Queens graduate. Indeed, a majority of the William and Mary professors and masters from 1729 to 1757 were Queens alumni.[2] Symbolic of the relationship was the dramatic appearance of President William Dawson and three of his full professors in complete Queens academic regalia on the occasion of the formal celebration of Transfer Day at William and Mary in 1747.[3] Dawson, in a letter to his friend, George Fothergill, chaplain of Queens, reported that after this ceremony, the quartet repaired to the common room and "cheerfully drank Prosperity to Col. Reg. Oxon."[4] The Queens relationship, moreover, was further strengthened through the person of another alumnus, Edmund Gibson, bishop of London. Gibson, as chancellor of William and Mary, was influential in matters of academic policy.

The link with Queens doubtless accentuated a need for improving the resources of the library in the area of classical literature. Student compositions, preserved among the Dawson papers in the Library of Congress, suggest a new emphasis on classical studies at the college after 1743. Dawson, it will be remembered, regretted in 1732 that the library lacked "a compleat set of the Classicks." And in 1738 that hard and fast theologian, President Blair, was still stubbornly resolved "to let the Classicks alone." It is therefore likely that after 1743 funds were earmarked to bridge those gaps in the library collection.

Insofar as finances were concerned, Blair left the library in good shape. Income from the tax on wines and liquors enabled the college authorities to make regular investments in books until the levy expired in 1776. The library was better off in this respect than most of its counterparts in England, where a regular income for academic libraries was the exception rather than the rule.[5] Eyewitness accounts of the conflagration of 1859, in which the book collection was consumed, stressed the loss of large numbers of volumes bearing the General Assembly bookplate, evidence that the volumes had been acquired with funds appropriated by the colonial legislature.[6]

The only colonial accounts of the college bursar that have been preserved commence in 1764. These list numerous expenditures on the part of the librarian, ranging in sums from one to sixty-two pounds.[7] Payments were made to several Williamsburg booksellers—such as Purdie and

Dixon and Thomas Dixon—but the entries are skimpy and do not spell out the titles that were acquired. Several loose invoices have also survived in the college archives showing that books were consigned to the college in 1765 and in 1771 by its London agents, C. and O. Hanbury and Osgood Hanbury and Company.[8] But, as usual, none of the volumes were listed by title. In general, it would be reasonable to assume that most of the library books were ordered from London. Yet bookstores were operating in Williamsburg. When William Parks, Virginia's first printer, decided to open a shop in 1742, the fact was carefully noted in the journal of the president and masters of the college.[9]

In 1761 the president and masters finally got around to appointing a librarian. Before this, as was noted earlier, the post was held by one of the grammar school ushers. But on June 26, 1761, Emanuel Jones, son of the earlier benefactor of the library, was formally appointed to the post.[10] Jones, who had been master of the Indian school since 1755, remained at the college until 1777.[11] In addition to serving as librarian, Jones acted as "Clerk to the Society," that is, secretary of the faculty.[12] The combination of these responsibilities continued in force at William and Mary well into the nineteenth century. As librarian, Jones received an annual salary of ten pounds sterling; as "Clerk to the Society," the sum of six pounds; and as master of the Indian school, approximately sixty pounds per annum drawn from the Brafferton revenues in England.[13]

Several entries in the Bursar's accounts between 1764 and 1770 suggest that Jones also handled the distribution of college textbooks.[14] This activity would have com-

menced in 1756 when the president and masters resolved
that

mr. Em: Jones be appointed to sell those Books wch the
Colledge shall imp[or] t—that he is not to stand to any Loss—
but sell them for seventy-five per cent: & be allowed ten per
cent: for his Trouble in selling & collecting.[15]

From 1743 until the outbreak of the American Revolution the library must have continued to enjoy the patronage of English friends of the college. It had become cus-
tomary for the various bishops of London and archbishops
of Canterbury, who alternated in the office of chancellor,
to contribute books to the collection. Tangible proof of
their benefactions would have disappeared in the fire of
1859. Nothing remains, for example, to show that Bishops
Sherlock and Hayter or Archbishops Herring, Hutton,
and Secker ever contributed to the collections. Nor is
there any surviving evidence that the only nonecclesias-
tical chancellors of the college during this period, the earls
of Hardwicke and of Egremont, made donations to the
library. But a failure to conform to precedent in this respect would have brought forth pointed reminders from
the academic officials.

The learned classicist, John Potter, archbishop of Canterbury from 1737 to 1747, presented to the library a
welcome addition to its church fathers, the great Benedic-
tine edition of the works of St. John Chrysostom.[16] Along
with this gift came Potter's own important two-volume
folio edition of *Clementis Alexandrini opera quae extant.*
And George III, soon after ascending the throne, donated
what was later described to his royal granddaughter as a
"superb copy of the authorized English version of the

Bible" in two volumes folio.[17] To all of this piety and learning, the naturalist Mark Catesby, who was well-known in Williamsburg, added his *Natural history of Carolina, Florida, and the Bahama Islands*.[18] Catesby's work, in two elephant folios with magnificent plates colored by the author, was highly prized by its custodians. Indeed, it was proudly displayed at every opportunity to visitors passing through Williamsburg. The text referred both to the college and to its Indian school. Thomas Jefferson, at some time or other during the course of his long association with William and Mary, carefully noted on a flyleaf that "it should never go out of the College."[19] It was among the most loudly bewailed treasures lost in the fire of 1859.

Colonial governors also continued the contributions to the library which their seventeenth-century predecessor, Colonel Nicholson, had taken such pains to encourage. Before departing for England in 1758, Governor Robert Dinwiddie—who "always looked on Seminaries of Learning with an awful respect and true Regard" and who held to the opinion that "the College of William and Mary is undoubtedly a very great Blessing to Virginia"[20]—turned over to the library the bulk of his personal collection of books.[21] Two of these miraculously escaped destruction both in 1859 and in 1862. One of the survivors is Dinwiddie's copy of Henry Grove's *System of moral philosophy* and the other is his copy of Felix Anthony de Alvarado's *Spanish and English dialogues: Containing an easy method of learning either of those languages*. The latter was far from the building when the fires of 1859 and 1862 took place. Luis Hue Girardin, an early nineteenth-century professor of modern languages at the college, removed

Alvarado at some time or other from the library shelves and added it to his own personal collection of books. Over Dinwiddie's elaborate armorial plate, the wayward professor casually pasted his own austere label. The book remained in the possession of Girardin's descendants until recovered by the college shortly after World War II. The subject matter of the volume is significant: it indicates that the library possessed some resources, at least, touching a field in which the college pioneered in 1779 with the establishment of the first American professorship of modern languages.

Gifts to the library occasionally arrived from unlikely sources. In 1747 John Sherwin, a seagoing friend of President Dawson, donated to the collection a copy of Benjamin Hederick's useful and popular *Graecum lexicon manuale* and a set of the two-volume folio edition of Anthony à Wood's *Athenae Oxoniensis*. Sherwin explained that he felt these "wou'd not ill suit a Colledge Library." The donation, recalling that of Captain Nicholas Humfrys in 1703/4, apparently stemmed from "the Genteel entertainment" which the donor received "from Mr. Dawson when at Williamsburg." In announcing the gift to Dawson, Sherwin expressed a hope that "you'l observe I am but a Voyager & accept this Mite, when I have a better Oportunity I shan't be mindful of something greater."[22]

The library also profited from the evangelical activities of the Society for the Propagation of the Gospel and the Society for the Propagation of Christian Knowledge. From 1742 to 1765 first William Dawson, then his brother Thomas, who succeeded Stith as president of the college in 1755, maintained active relations with the two organizations. Virtually all of the letters directed by the Dawson brothers to the officials of the two societies mention the distribution of pious literature.[23] Many of the books dispatched to evangelical arenas by the SPG and the SPCK probably ended up on the college shelves. The hapless students paid in sweat and tears for this flood of inspiration and devotion. On July 12, 1744, for instance, William Dawson advised Philip Bearcroft, secretary of the SPG, that he had received 150 copies of the Bishop of Sodor and Man's (that is, Thomas Wilson's) *Essay towards an instruction for the Indians.* That tract, begun at Oglethorpe's insistence and dedicated to Georgia's trustees, carried a commendatory preface written by Dawson himself. Dawson notified Bearcroft that a copy was given to each "of our Scholars," who were employed "every Night last Lent, in reading audibly, distinctly and solemnly, so much of this excellent Work, as the Understandings of the Hearers, in general, were able to receive."[24]

One of the most unusual accessions made by the library in the years immediately preceding the American Revolution was drawn from the estate of Rev. James Horrocks. Horrocks, holder of a master of arts degree from Trinity, Cambridge, and one-time usher at Wakefield School in England, had come to Virginia in 1762 to serve as master of the grammar school at William and Mary.[25] In 1764, amid some bitterness within the faculty, he succeeded Rev. William Yates as president of the college. Death came to Horrocks while he was en route to England in 1771. The following year, the college selected and purchased from the deceased president's effects a small but choice collection of volumes that were wanted on its library shelves.

Samuel Henley, who had joined the faculty in 1770 as professor of moral philosophy and who later acquired dubious distinction in translating William Beckford's *Vathek*, apparently assumed the task of selecting the books for the college.[26] An inventory of Henley's selections, in his own hand and dated December 8, 1772, is still preserved in the college archives.[27] The list of titles exhibits a shift in emphasis at the college from theology and the classics to the physical sciences. Indeed, the books purchased from the Horrocks estate, costing £17/12/—, reflected the impact of entirely new intellectual ideals. This shift must be attributed in part to the lectures of Professor William Small, a man described by Jefferson, one of his students, as "profound in most of the useful branches of science."[28] Small's lectures at William and Mary from 1758 to 1764 stressed disciplines that in a decade or so were to become dominant features of the curriculum.

Foremost among the works selected by Henley from the Horrocks collection was that indispensable adjunct to eighteenth-century enlightened thought, a set of Pierre Bayle's *Dictionnaire historique et critique*. As Professor Fraser Neiman notes in his introduction to *The Henley-Horrocks inventory*, Horrocks' set of Bayle may have been in French or in English, for the entry in Henley's inventory fails to specify the edition. Of equal significance is the fact that the Horrocks accession brought to the college shelves two of Sir Isaac Newton's greatest works, his *Principia mathematica* and his *Opticks*, as well as a copy of his *Universal arithmetick*. Another major work in its field, Guillaume François de L'Hôpital's *Method of fluxions*, was among the volumes acquired from the deceased president's effects.

Other works in mathematics came from the same source. These included the three-volume quarto edition of Thomas Simpson's *Miscellaneous tracts* and Simpson's textbook on *Elements of plane geometry*, copies of William Emerson's *Arithmetick of infinities*, Nicholas Saunderson's *Elements of algebra*, Luke Trevigar's *Sectionum conicarum elementa*, John Ward's *Compendium of algebra*, Henry Gore's *Elements of solid geometry*, and James Hodgson's textbook on *The doctrine of fluxions*.

Astronomy was represented in Henley's selections by the works of James Ferguson, a dominant figure in eighteenth-century astronomical research; these included Ferguson's most influential production, *Astronomy explained*, which went through thirteen editions before 1811, his popular *Lectures on select subjects in mechanics*, and his *Tables and tracts*. Two works on navigation—Archibald Patoun's *Complete treatise of navigation* and William Emerson's *Mathematical principles of geography*—together with copies of Charles Leadbetter's *Mechanick dialling* and Richard Jack's *Mathematical principles of theology* also appeared on the Henley list. Another entry covered several unspecified pamphlets and three untitled "calendeiers." The latter may have been almanacs or, as Professor Neiman has suggested, tables of considerable substance inasmuch as they cost the college nine shillings.

But the most notable components of the accession, aside from Bayle's great dictionary and Newton's major works, were in the fields of physics and electrical research. Interest in these areas had been promoted at William and Mary by Small's lectures and by the laboratory equipment that Small had purchased for the college in England in 1767. Horrocks had obviously been intrigued by the same subjects, for his private library contained copies—acquired by Henley for the college—of Benjamin Franklin's *Experiments and observations on electricity*, Joseph Priestley's *History and present state of electricity*, and Benjamin Wilson's *Short view of electricity*. In short, a useful collection of treatises reflecting contemporary scientific thought was added to the shelves of a library that had previously stressed theology and the classics.

The other volumes in Horrocks' extensive private library were sold in Williamsburg, according to the August 13, 1772, *Virginia gazette*, "at Mr. William Pearce's Store . . . where Catalogues, with the Prices annexed, may be seen." No copy of the catalogue is known to have survived. But at least one volume thus dispersed—Volume II of Croker, Williams, and Clark's *Complete dictionary of arts and sciences*—has come to light within recent years and has been given to the college. The fact that this work was dismissed by Henley in making his selections for the library may indicate that a set of the multivolume compilation was already on the college shelves in 1772.

The mid-eighteenth-century development of book collections within the frameworks of undergraduate societies and clubs is indicative of the limited role allotted the library in the life of the academic community. Its stately folios and ponderous sets of patristical, theological, and philosophical lore, as well as any lighter resources in the fields of art, history, belles-lettres, the classics, and biography, were assembled solely for the use of the masters and graduate students. The undergraduate was expected to form his own personal shelf of books for general and recreational reading. If a youth fancied the lively works of the restoration dramatists or the witticisms of Alexander Pope, he had to acquire the volumes either from a dealer in Williamsburg or through his family's London agent.

But valuing good fellowship, a group of William and Mary students in 1750 banded together and organized the first undergraduate fraternity thus far discovered in the annals of an American university or college.[29] The members, in their private correspondence, secretly referred to the organization as "the F.H.C. Society." It is now generally believed that the initials, despite the redundancy of the resulting phrase, stood for Flat Hat Club. Miss Jane Carson, writing in the Thomas Perkins Abernethy *festschrift* entitled *The Old Dominion* (1964), which was edited by Darrett B. Rutman, has suggested, on the other hand, that the initials could just as well have stood for *Fraternitas Hilaritas Cognitioque*. In any event, the F.H.C. Society sought to develop a library for the edification of its brethren.

Undergraduate societies founded later in the century at other academic establishments were motivated by similar aims. At Harvard, for example, both the Hasty Pudding and Porcellian clubs undertook the development of book collections. The Harvard fraternities kept their respective collections in an undergraduate librarian's room, affording the members "an opportunity of general reading for which the College Library was then ill-equipped."[30]

The F.H.C. Society from about 1770 to 1776 enjoyed

the patronage of Thomas Gwatkin, a Christ Church, Oxford, master of arts who had come to William and Mary in 1770 as professor of natural philosophy and mathematics.[31] Gwatkin was requested by the brethren to prepare a catalogue of "the most useful and valuable books with which it would be proper to begin the establishment of a Library."[32] In complying, Gwatkin provided posterity with a glimpse of what was considered good undergraduate reading matter at the college on the eve of the American Revolution. He listed his recommendations under six headings: (1) moral philosophy and civil law, (2) mathematics, natural philosophy, and natural history, (3) history, (4) government, (5) trade, and, of course, (6) miscellaneous works.[33] As proof of his familiarity with the works thus cited, he arranged the titles under each heading according to the size of the volumes, folio, quarto, octavo, and duodecimo.

Many of the works proposed by Gwatkin for the F.H.C. Society must have duplicated works already on the college library shelves. For example, Newton's *Principia*, listed in the section on mathematics, natural philosophy, and natural history, had been purchased from the Horrocks estate. Newton's *Opticks*, Priestley's *Electricity*, and Simpson's *Geometry*, also proposed by Gwatkin, had come from the same source. And Burnet's celebrated *History of the reformation*, a F.H.C. Society desideratum, had probably been given to the college by the author himself.

The emphasis on mathematics and the physical sciences noted in connection with the books that Samuel Henley had selected from Horrocks' effects was even more pronounced in the fraternity checklist. Nearly 50 per cent of the titles touched those subjects. This means that the impressive sets of theological and classical literature that were gathered on the college shelves had virtually assumed the status of antiquarian memorabilia. The college itself, as a matter of fact, was in the throes of an intellectual ferment that was to culminate, during the American Revolution, in a drastic revision of its academic organization and aims.

CHAPTER FIVE

A Good Foundation to Improve Upon
1776–1793

THE departure in 1776 and 1777 of several Tory members of the faculty signaled the dissolution of ties that had bound the college to its English supporters and to English academic thought and precedent since 1693. The severance of these links was not altogether unheralded, for spirited conflicts had marred relations between the native-born visitors of the college and its Oxford-bred faculty since the middle of the century.[1] Any attempt to relate the library to this intracollegiate struggle, however, would give undue emphasis to the library's role in the life of the academic community. Innovations adopted shortly after 1776 nevertheless suggest that liberal elements within the collegiate establishment had already prepared the ground for possible modifications to the library program.

A preview of the possible impact of revolutionary hostilities on the library collections came in June 1776 when a representative of the Virginia Convention appeared at the college gates, armed with a commission to determine whether or not the main academic building could be converted into "a proper hospital for the reception and accommodation of sick and wounded soldiers."[2] After touring the premises, and presumably conferring with Librarian Emanuel Jones and other officials, the commissioner concluded that quarters for the proposed hospital would have to be sought somewhere else. The convention was advised that the structure, by reason of numerous partitions, would not admit proper circulation of air, that it was already prepared for the reception of "scholars" scheduled to return to classes the following week, and that the "large and valuable library" might be damaged by removal, "perhaps totally ruined."[3]

Despite the turmoil and confusion of the times, the college succeeded in maintaining an uninterrupted academic schedule from 1776 until the spring of 1781. But the siege of Yorktown in 1781 thrust Williamsburg into the main theater of military operations. Classes and lectures were thereupon suspended, and the three principal college buildings—the main structure, the Brafferton or Indian school, and the President's house—were requisitioned for military purposes. The library collections, left in the main building, were subjected during this interval to pillage and vandalism by the British, French, and American troops who were alternately quartered on the premises. Specific details respecting the damages and losses that were sustained are not revealed in the surviving records. But Richard Randolph, in drafting a claim for damages which was laid before the Virginia General Assembly in 1839, asserted that "many of the books were lost, and the apparatus [that is, the highly prized laboratory equipment that Professor Small had purchased for the college in England in 1767] seriously injured."[4]

On April 9, 1777, a significant break with the past oc-

7. Governor Robert Dinwiddie's bookplate, overlaid with Luis Hue Girardin's nineteenth-century book label, in Felix Anthony de Alvarado's *Spanish and English dialogues*, one of a collection of books presented by Dinwiddie to the College of William and Mary in 1758. (Courtesy of College of William and Mary)

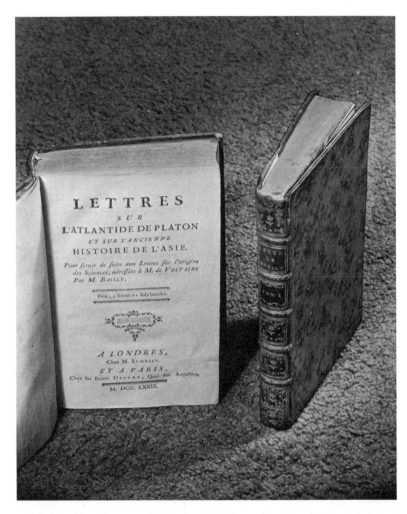

8. Books presented to the College of William and Mary by Louis XVI of France. (Courtesy of College of William and Mary)

curred when Emanuel Jones, probably angry and bewildered by changes that beset the college, either willingly or unwillingly "resigned . . . as Clerk of the Meeting & Librarian."[5] Rev. John Bracken, "into whose hands the Key of the Library &c were delivered," was appointed on the same date to serve as Jones's successor. Bracken, confronted with a problem that has plagued library keepers since time immemorial, shortly thereafter inserted the following notice in Alexander Purdie's *Virginia gazette*:

It is earnestly requested of all Gentlemen who have any books belonging to the College library in their possession, to return the same immediately.[6]

The plea was repeated a week later in Dixon and Hunter's *Virginia gazette*.[7]

The election in 1777 of Rev. James Madison, a cousin of the statesman of the same name, to succeed the Tory John Camm as president of the college marked a complete break with the past. Madison, the first alumnus of William and Mary to occupy the post, represented a background and ideals closely allied to those of his friend and associate, Thomas Jefferson.[8] In cooperation with Jefferson, Madison was to be responsible for effecting revolutionary changes in the organization and curriculum of the college.

Jefferson, as one of the revisors charged in 1776 with revamping the laws of Virginia, drafted a scheme of general education for the state that embraced three levels of instruction: "elementary schools for all children generally, rich and poor"; colleges "for a middle degree of instruction, calculated for the common purposes of life"; and a university "for teaching the sciences generally, & in their highest degree."⁹ In a bill especially designed to meet the last object, Jefferson sought "to amend the constitution of Wm. & Mary College, to enlarge its sphere of science, and to make it in fact an University."¹⁰ By this measure he hoped to convert his alma mater into a state-supported university and to secularize an establishment that, in his words, was "purely of the Church of England."¹¹

But the bill was never enacted into law. It is cited here because it embraced a program for the collection of research materials for the college library that was far in advance of its time. The bill, as drafted by Jefferson, would have abolished the Indian school attached to the college and would have substituted therefor "a perpetual mission among the Indian tribes." This, to be sure, would have respected the requirement of the Brafferton trustees that the Indians be instructed in the principles of Christianity. But, as Professor Julian P. Boyd has observed, an object that must have been uppermost in Jefferson's mind was that of having the missionary to the Indians "collect their traditions, laws, customs, languages, and other circumstances." Jefferson's bill for reconstituting the college stipulated that the missionary should

communicate, from time to time to the said president and professors [of William and Mary] the materials he collects to be by them laid up and preserved in their library, for which trouble the said missionary shall be allowed a salary at the discretion of the visitors out of the revenues of the college.

Jefferson, in other words, was prepared to transform the college library from a depository of printed books into a respository of original source materials.

Though Jefferson's bill for amending the charter of the college was never enacted into law, its author, shortly after becoming governor of Virginia on June 1, 1779, was elected to the college board of visitors. In the latter capacity, Jefferson succeeded in effecting many of the revolutionary changes in the college organization and curriculum that were originally proposed in his unsuccessful bid to amend the charter. On December 4, 1779, acting in cooperation with James Madison, the college president, Jefferson induced the board of visitors to abolish the grammar school and the two chairs of divinity and in their place to introduce chairs of modern languages, of anatomy, medicine, and chemistry, and of law and police. The duties of the professor of moral philosophy were broadened to cover both "the Law of Nature and Nations" and the fine arts, and those of the professor of mathematics and natural philosophy to include natural history. An elective system of study was also adopted. The college was thereupon designated a university.[12]

A few weeks later, on December 29, 1779, the president and faculty issued the first rules for the government of the college library thus far discovered in the institutional archives. It was resolved that no professor would be allowed to keep books drawn from the collection for more than six months and that all loans would have to be properly entered against the borrowers' names in a register provided for that purpose.[13] John Bracken's 1777 notice in the *Virginia gazette* had indicated that a slipshod system for recording loans left the librarian uninformed as to the whereabouts of his charges. The librarian was also directed by the faculty on December 29, 1779, to submit thereafter an annual report on the state of the library, "immediately after the Christmas vacation."

On December 30 the faculty turned its attention to even more fundamental problems confronting the library. The income that the library had enjoyed since 1734 from the provincial duty on alcoholic imports was abruptly terminated in 1776 upon the establishment of the Commonwealth. This does not mean that abstinence accompanied independence: the colonial levy simply expired and authority for its renewal was not exercised by a reconstituted Virginia General Assembly. Independence from the mother country also cost the college other lucrative sources of revenue. The Brafferton estate in Yorkshire, the income from which had been diverted at times to library purposes, was confiscated by the English Crown. In consequence, funds for improving the book collection were not available. Jefferson vainly sought to remedy this deficiency by substituting more certain revenues for the support of the college in his unsuccessful measure aimed at amending its charter.

Regulations, or policy, that limited the use of the library to the masters and graduate students, moreover, were inconsistent with the republican sentiments that motivated Jefferson and Madison in their reorganization of the college in 1779. Perhaps each, as an undergraduate, had suffered the frustration of being denied access to the book collection. Jefferson after 1776 was actually contemplating, in his package of bills aimed at creating a general system of education for the state, the establishment of a "Public Library" for "indulging the researches of the learned and curious."[14]

In consequence, moved both by the necessity for raising funds and by a determination to open the library to all students, graduate and undergraduate alike, the president and faculty on December 30, 1779, resolved that

the Ceremony of Matriculation shall be a pecuniary Contribution to the Library, from every Student when he enters the College & annually afterwards, on which his Name together with his Contribution shall be entered in a Book kept for that Purpose by the Bursar, & he shall be entitled to the Use of the Library.[15]

The matriculation fee was set at ten shillings per annum. One third of the total proceeds therefrom was appropriated to the administration of the library; the remaining two thirds were to be "laid out in purchasing Books."

The president and faculty on December 30, 1779, also directed Librarian John Bracken to arrange the library collections "according to the different Branches of Literature." It is not known what classification rules or methods of physical arrangement had previously been employed. In 1779 the books were obviously not arranged according to subject matter. In all probability the folios, quartos, octavos, and duodecimos, regardless of content, had been standing on shelves allocated to their respective heights. Or perhaps the integrity of the various donations had been maintained by shelving the books according to provenance in presses carrying the donor's name blazoned over the doors as in Duke Humphrey's library at the Bodleian. The William and Mary officials had certainly toyed with this notion in their 1732 plans for diverting the income from Boyle's bequest to the purchase of books. Speculation on cataloguing methods would be even more futile, for even

the English and Scottish universities were notoriously back-
ward in this respect throughout the eighteenth century.[16]

As a result of the decision to reclassify the resources of
the library, all of the books in circulation were recalled on
May 20, 1780.[17] On the same date Charles Bellini, Jefferson's friend and protegé who occupied the chair of modern languages, was elected to succeed John Bracken as
librarian. Abbé Claude Robin, finding the college tempo-
rarily closed when he passed through Williamsburg en
route to Yorktown in September 1781, met Bellini and
flatteringly observed:

Nous n'avons retrouvé qu'un seul Professeur, Italien d'origine; son esprit, son savoir nous font, d'après ce qu'il nous a
dit de ses Confrères, regretter leur eloignement.[18]

The conversations between Robin and Bellini may have
taken place in the library, "une bibliothèque d'environ
trois mille volumes," for Robin was moved when

j'ai contemplé avec un intérêt bien vif ces vrais monumens de
la gloire des hommes; en me rappelant des momens heureux,
ils me rappeloient des personnes chères à mon coeur. Le
tumulte des armes a fait fuir ceux qui en faisoient usage; les
Muses, vous le savez, ne se plaisent que dans le séjour de la
paix.[19]

The faculty on May 20, 1780, resolved to provide Bellini with explicit instructions governing the circulation of
books. It decided that

none of the Books be hereafter delivered out of the Library
to any but Professors & matriculated Students and to them for
one month only at a Time; when they shall be returned,

otherwise the Borrower shall not only be accountable for the value of the Book withheld, but be deprived of the Priviledge untill the Society upon proper amends at a subsequent Meeting agree to restore it . . . If any borrowed Book be defaced, torn or otherwise injured, he who had the use of it shall replace it by another of the same Author, equal to what it was when first put into his hands . . . The first Monday in every Month at 9 oclock Morning is appointed as a Time to receive all Books lent out.[20]

The 1780 library regulations were subsequently expanded and incorporated in the college statutes, and published with them in 1792.[21] This was the first appearance in print of any rules and regulations devised for the management of the book collection. Section VI of the statutes stipulated:

1. No Student shall be priviledged to take any books from the library, who hath not first paid ten shillings to the Bursar, and produced a receipt of such payment to the Librarian, which sum shall entitle the Student to the use of the library for one year.

2. No Student shall receive more than one book at a time; the value of which he shall previously deposit with the Librarian.

3. Every Student taking a book, shall regularly return it to the Librarian in the Council Chamber, within one month at farthest; otherwise he shall be deprived of the use of the library.

4. No Student shall apply for a book, except on Mondays and Fridays, and then application shall be made to the Librarian, between the hours of nine and ten in the morning.

5. Every Student losing, defacing or in any way injuring a book belonging to the library, shall forfeit the deposit made on receiving the book; and if such book be lost, and be part

of a set, he shall forfeit the full value of the set, or replace the book.

In short, on the eve of its centennial the library, though open to all matriculates, was safeguarded by a somewhat formidable array of rules and regulations governing the circulation of books.

In accessions, the contrast between the colonial period and the period after 1776 was accentuated by several donations received in 1783 and 1784. Before the American Revolution the library had enjoyed the patronage of English kings, archbishops, bishops, royal governors, and men of letters. But a procession of French visitors passing through Williamsburg during and immediately after the Revolutionary conflict ignited a smoldering admiration for France and for French intellectual thought. One of Jefferson's proudest accomplishments was the introduction of French into the college curriculum in 1779. And in 1782 the college was pleased to bestow honorary degrees on two distinguished French guests, the marquis de Chastellux and Jean-François Coste. Chastellux, in recording his impressions of the college, reported that "if miracles need be cited to enhance her fame, [I might add] that she has made me a Doctor of Law!"[22] As a token of his gratitude Chastellux in 1783 presented to the library a set of his two-volume work entitled *De la félicité publique*.[23]

Chastellux was instrumental in 1784 in obtaining for the library a substantial gift of books donated in the name of Louis XVI of France. The French Minister of Foreign Affairs, the comte de Vergennes, joined Chastellux in soliciting the donation, which was transmitted to the college through the good offices of François Barbé-Marbois, secre-

tary of the French Legation in Philadelphia. The royal gift
—"deux cents volumes des plus beaux et des meilleurs
ouvrages français"—arrived in New York City in July
1784 on board the French packet *Courier de l'Amérique*,
and from thence was shipped overland to Virginia. But

le négociant de Richmond qui était chargé de les faire passer
au collège, a oublié assez longtems dans sa cave milieu des
barrils de sucre et d'huile, pour les avoir remis absolument
gâtés.[24]

The books reached the college at the end of the year. If the
condition of the two volumes still in the possession of the
library is indicative of the condition in which the rest of
the volumes were received, the books did not suffer great
ill effects from their sojourn in the Richmond warehouse.

The comte de Vergennes, in responding to President
Madison's acknowledgment of the gift, politely explained
that

Le Roi a eu une véritable satisfaction á vous envoyer la petite
collection de livres dont vous accusez la réception; elle ne
saurait être mieux placée que dans la bibliothèque d'une uni-
versité aussi distinguée que celle que vous possédez; et Sa
Majesté se flatte que vous la regarderez toujour comme une
marque de sa bienveillance et de son affection pour votres
estimable corps.[25]

Unfortunately, as previously noted, only two out of the
two hundred volumes donated by "his most Christian Majesty" survived the disastrous conflagration of 1859.

The University of Pennsylvania was also a recipient, at
the same time, of a collection of books donated in the name
of Louis XVI.[26] Happily, the Pennsylvania consignment,
thirty-six titles in one hundred volumes, has been pre-

served almost intact. Professor Howard C. Rice, noting the presence in the Pennsylvania lot of several of the marquis de Chastellux's favorite authors—Buffon, Tacitus, and Metastasio, for example—has concluded that Chastellux had a hand in making the selections.[27] As might be expected, moreover, many of the books were printed in Paris at "la Imprimerie Royale."

On the basis of what little is known about the volumes comprising the gift to William and Mary, there is reason for believing that one half of the collection duplicated the one hundred volumes sent to Pennsylvania. The only two volumes that have survived, copies of Jean Sylvain Bailly's *Lettres sur l'origine des sciences* and *Lettres sur l'Atlantide de Platon et sur l'ancienne histoire de Asie*, duplicate, for example, works that were donated to Pennsylvania. And both institutions were favored with sets of Georges Louis Leclerc Buffon's monumental *Histoire naturelle*.[28] A large percentage of the works given to Pennsylvania touched scientific subjects. This also characterized the donation to William and Mary, for President Madison told the comte de Vergennes:

Our attachment to a Nation so peculiarly distinguished for its Emminence in Science hath always been great, but it can not fail to become still more close and intimate, since we have experienced so generous and noble a Desire to disseminate a Portion of that Science even amongst us.[29]

As the work by Buffon would suggest, another segment of the gift to Pennsylvania stressed French interest in natural history. Copies of the same works must have been in the much larger collection of books presented to William and Mary, for George Tucker, who inspected the library in 1816, "noticed with great pleasure a donation of many volumes, chiefly Natural History, presented by our unfortunate Louis XVI."[30] In short, it is believed that the components of the Pennsylvania collection, all of which are known by title, were duplicated in the consignment to William and Mary.

The French gift, in consequence, would have brought to the William and Mary shelves copies of such works in the field of scientific inquiry as the marquis de Courtanvaux's *Journal du voyage . . . pour essayer, par ordre de l'Académie, plusieurs instrumens relatifs à la longitude*, Christoph Delius' *Traité sur la science de l'exploitation des mines*, Philippe de la Hire's *Divers ouvrages de mathématique et de physique*, Jacques Dortous de Mairan's *Traité physique et historique de l'aurore boréale*, and a compilation of essays entitled *Recueil d'observations faites en plusieurs voyages . . . pour perfectionner l'astronomie et la géographie*.

Natural history was represented by copies of Jean de la Marck's *Flore françoise*, Jean Soulavie's *Histoire naturelle de la France méridionale*, René Réaumur's *Memoires pour servir à l'histoire des insectes*, and, of course, Buffon's multivolume *Histoire naturelle*.

As might be expected of a collection of books assembled in Paris, the French gift also embraced a representative array of studies inspired by the history of France. The royal donor's lineage was appropriately recalled by copies of such works as Joseph Desormeaux' *Histoire de la maison de Bourbon*, Guillaume de Jaligny's *Histoire de Charles VIII*, and Jean de Joinville's *Histoire de Saint Louis*. The glory of the royal house was further exhibited in such volumes as Charles Le Brun's *Grande galerie de Versailles* and Charles Lubersac de Livron's *Discours sur le monumens publics de tous les âges . . . suivi d'une description de monument projeté à la gloire de Louis XVI & de la France.*

Volume I—the only volume in print in 1784—of *L'art de vérifier les dates des faits historiques, des chartes, des chroniques, et autres anciens monumens,* one of the great landmarks of eighteenth-century French scholarship, headed the general historical works. These included copies of Philippe d'Arcq's *Histoire générale des guerres,* Jean Philippe René de La Bléterie's translation of the *Annales* of Tacitus, the important *Annales* of Joannes Zonaras, and the *Byzantina historia* of Nicephorus Gregoras.

Travel and description accounted for still another segment of the royal gift. The works in this field included, for example, copies of Marc Bourrit's *Description des Alpes, Pennines et Rhetiennes* and Jean d'Anville's *Mémoires sur l'Egypte ancienne et moderne.* But the loss of the French collection in the fire of 1859, together with the loss of any checklist that might have been compiled covering its components, has effectively obliterated all traces of at least one hundred of the two hundred volumes comprising the gift.

Another post-Revolutionary benefactor of the library was that bird of exotic plumage, John Paradise, the friend of Samuel Johnson, James Boswell, Benjamin Franklin, and Thomas Jefferson. Paradise, married to Lucy Ludwell, a great-granddaughter of one of the original trustees of the college, removed from London to Virginia in 1787 in order to manage his wife's extensive Virginia estates. Warmly welcomed in Williamsburg, Paradise was immediately admitted into a congenial circle of intellectuals that included such college officials as President Madison, Professor of Law George Wythe, and Librarian Charles Bellini.[31] Under these auspices Paradise was elected in 1787, shortly after his arrival in Virginia, to the college board of visitors. Evidence that Paradise—a "man of letters and true gentleman," according to Bellini—donated books to the library came to light in 1928 with the discovery in a privately owned manuscript collection of a fragmented title page bearing the inscription "Presented by John Paradise to the University of William and Mary."[32] But the fragment was so imperfect that even Librarian Earl Gregg Swem was unable to determine the title and subject of the work.

A gift to the library bringing to mind the days of Rev. James Blair arrived in 1783 from the ancient Dr. Thomas Wilson, "of Bath in Great Britain."[33] Dr. Wilson, though an eminent book collector, chose to favor the college with the somewhat tedious evangelical works of his own father, Thomas Wilson, the celebrated bishop of Sodor and Man. Even in resolving to "address in a Letter to Dr. Wilson the sense they have of so valuable an addition to the Library," the faculty was inventing empty phrases. Not a single divinity student had been admitted since 1779. A disturbed Jedidiah Morse informed Ezra Stiles of Yale in 1786 that

Doctor Madison is Professor Divinity, but he never exhibits Lectures upon it.–because there is not one Student, nor hasn't been a number of years, that has any Idea of making Divinity his Study.–Such, however incredible, is the State of William and Mary College.[34]

And a worldly alumnus, Isaac Coles, writing to Henry St. George Tucker toward the end of the century upon the latter's graduation from William and Mary, recalled that

the spirit of skepticism which so much prevailed & which every student acquired as soon as he touched the threshhold of the college is certainly the first step towards knowledge; it puts the mind in a proper state not only to receive, but also to receive correctly. That it leads to Deism, atheism &c I will acknowledge, but on the same grounds we may object to reason.[35]

Madison, though serving after 1790 not only as president of the college but also as bishop of Virginia, was primarily interested in scientific pursuits. La Rochefoucauld, who visited the college in 1796, was struck by the richness of the personal library that "l'évêque Madisson" had collected "en physique, en chimie, et même en littérature." The Frenchman noted:

Sa bibliothèque, bien moins nombreuse que celle du collège, est composée de livres d'un meilleur choix, sur-tout parmi ceux relatifs aux sciences. Il augmente annuellement sa collection des ouvrages savans et nouveaux les plus estimes.[36]

Madison's efforts to develop the college library were thwarted, of course, by the loss of income which the college sustained when funds from England were cut off during the American Revolution. Ezra Stiles, the president of Yale, opening a "fraternal communication" with Madison in 1780, confided that he was convinced "the present Revolution in America will necessitate us to collect & embosom the Literature of the Universe."[37] Madison cheerfully concurred and cautiously advised his colleague that "our [William and Mary] Library may be considered as a good foundation to improve upon."[38] Madison, in the same letter, explained that before

this unnatural War, we had formed a Plan of importing annually some of the best modern Books, and among the others the Publications of the different Philosophical Societies in Europe, which we shall resume whenever it is practicable.

As previously noted, the college in 1779 levied a matriculation fee of ten shillings a student for the support of the library and allocated two thirds of the total proceeds annually to the purchase of books. But the student body in the years immediately following the American Revolution seldom exceeded sixty to seventy students, so the funds available for library acquisitions never exceeded a paltry £23 per annum. The deficiencies in the library collections noted by La Rochefoucauld in 1796 substantiate the surmise that Madison's plans for importing "the best modern Books" floundered on the shoals of inadequate financing.

Even so, despite the destruction of its original holdings in the fire of 1705, the library in 1781, contained some three thousand volumes.[39] It was, in consequence, the second largest academic book repository in the new republic. The Harvard collection at that time numbered approximately twelve thousand volumes, Yale had around twenty-seven hundred, and Princeton fifteen hundred.[40] When the college celebrated its centennial anniversary in 1793, the library collection, thanks mainly to the gift of Louis XVI, would have increased to approximately four thousand volumes.

Virtually all of the visitors or commentators who recorded their observations at the college during the last decades of the eighteenth century were impressed by the library. Chastellux noted in 1782 that the college

is a magnificent establishment which adorns Williamsburg and does honor to Virginia. The beauty of the building is surpassed by the richness of the library, and the worth of this library by several of the distinguished professors, such as Doctors Madison, Wythe, Bellini, etc., etc., who may be looked upon as living books, in which both precepts and examples are to be found.[41]

Jedidiah Morse on his circuit of the southern states in 1786, though shocked by the low state of interest in theology and religion at William and Mary, told Ezra Stiles of Yale that "their Library, like ours, is well stocked with Ancient Authors."[42] Edmund Randolph, writing to Alexander Addison of Philadelphia in 1792, alluded to William and Mary's "admirable library, containing the most rare gems of ancient learning."[43] And La Rochefoucauld, a guest at the college in 1796, noted that it "possède une bibliothèque assez bien fournie de livres classiques; presque tous sont de vieux livres, à l'exception de deux cents volumes . . . envoyés en présent par Louis XVI."[44]

The surviving evidence relating to the growth of the book collection and the management and utilization of the library during its first one hundred years, 1693–1793, is obviously slender. President Madison, who knew the library as well if not better than anyone else, must therefore be given the last word: he concluded, on the eve of its centennial, that it was "a good foundation to improve upon."

NOTES

NOTES

CHAPTER ONE
The Founding of the College, 1617–1693

1. For evidence concerning the Henrico project, see H. B. Adams, *The College of William and Mary* (U.S. Bureau of Education, Circulars of information, No. 1: Washington, D.C.: Gov't print. off., 1887), p. 11; R. H. Land, "Henrico and its college," *William and Mary quarterly* (hereafter abbreviated to *WMQ*), 2d ser., XVIII (1938), 453–498; P. A. Bruce, *Institutional history of Virginia in the seventeenth century* (New York: G. P. Putnam's sons, 1910), I, 362–373; E. D. Neill, *The history of education in Virginia during the seventeenth century* (Washington, D.C.: Gov't print. off., 1867), *passim;* E. D. Neill, *Virginia vetusta* (Albany, N.Y.: J. Munsell's sons, 1885), pp. 167–168; J. S. Flory, "The University of Henrico," *Southern History Association Publications*, VIII (1904), 40–52; and L. G. Tyler, *The College of William and Mary* (Richmond: Whittet & Shepperson, 1907), pp. 3–5.

2. Land, *op. cit.*, p. 483.

3. For evidence touching the East India School, see Land, *op. cit., passim;* Bruce, *op. cit.*, I, 346–349; Neill, *Virginia vetusta*, p. 179; and Tyler, *op. cit.*, p. 4.

4. Land, *op. cit.*, p. 486.

5. *Ibid.*, p. 487.

6. Hellmut Lehmann-Haupt, *The book in America* (New York: R. R. Bowker co., 1939), p. 355.

7. Susan M. Kingsbury, ed., *Records of the Virginia Company of London* (Washington, D.C.: Gov't print. off., 1906–1935), I, 421–422.

8. *Ibid.*, p. 589.

9. *Ibid.*, p. 421.

10. Neill, *Virginia vetusta*, pp. 172 173.

11. E. L. Goodwin, *The colonial church in Virginia* (Milwaukee: Morehouse publishing co., [1927]), p. 248.

12. Land, *op. cit.*, p. 493.

13. *Ibid.*, p. 497.

14. Adams, *op. cit.*, p. 12. For other evidence on the Palmer scheme, see Bruce, *op. cit.*, I, 372–373; Neill, *Virginia vetusta*, pp. 182–184; and Tyler, *op. cit.*, p. 5.

15. Bruce, *op. cit., passim*, and P. A. Bruce, *Economic history of Virginia in the seventeenth century* (New York: Macmillan co., 1907), *passim*.

16. Bruce, *Economic history*, I, 319, 336. See also C. M. Andrews, *The colonial period of American history* (New Haven: Yale university press, 1934), I, 237.

17. Bruce, *Economic history*, I, 397.

18. T. E. Keys, "The colonial library and the development of sectional differences in the American colonies," *Library quarterly*, VIII (1938), 383. See also William Peden, "Some notes concerning Thomas Jefferson's libraries," *WMQ*, 3d ser., I (1944), 265.

19. Adams, *op. cit.*, p. 12.
20. Bruce, *Institutional history*, I, 375.
21. Adams, *op. cit.*, p. 13.
22. *The charter, transfer, and statutes of the college of William and Mary* (Williamsburg, Va.: William Hunter, 1758), p. 113. See also Adams, *op. cit.*, p. 14.
23. See E. G. Swem's "James Blair," *Dictionary of American biography* (hereafter abbreviated to *DAB*), II, 335–336. See also Goodwin, *op. cit.*, p. 251, and Tyler, *op. cit.*, p. 7.
24. See L. W. Labaree, "Francis Nicholson," *DAB*, XIII, 499–502.
25. Bruce, *Institutional history*, I, 381.
26. Tyler, *op. cit.*, p. 8.
27. *Charter, transfer, and statutes*, p. 110.
28. *Ibid.*, p. 5.
29. Adams, *op. cit.*, pp. 16–17.
30. Tyler, *op. cit.*, pp. 9–10.
31. *Charter, transfer, and statutes*, p. 45.
32. *Ibid.*, pp. 47–61.
33. Adams, *op. cit.*, p. 15.
34. See James Blair to Francis Nicholson, December 3, 1691, in *Virginia magazine of history and biography* (hereafter abbreviated to *VMH&B*), VII (1899), 160–163.
35. *Ibid.*
36. *Ibid.*
37. A discussion of the curriculum can be found in L. G. Tyler, "From the records of William and Mary College," *Papers of the American Historical Association* (New York and London: G. P. Putnam's sons, 1890), IV, 455–460. See also T. J. Wertenbaker, *The old South* (New York: Scribner's, 1942), p. 33, and *The charter, transfer, and statutes*.
38. *Charter, transfer, and statutes*, pp. 135–137.
39. *Ibid.*, pp. 6–7, 29–37.
40. *Ibid.*, pp. 31–37.
41. Tyler, *College of William and Mary*, p. 13.

CHAPTER TWO
The First Book Collection, 1693–1705

1. James Blair to Francis Nicholson, December 3, 1691, in *VMH&B*, VII (1899), 160–163.
2. *WMQ*, 1st ser., XIX (1910–11), 42.
3. Blair's accounts are printed in [Francis Nicholson], *Papers relating to an affadavit* (London, 1727), pp. 68–72.

4. Consult arrangements for shipment of books mentioned in letter of James Blair to Thomas Tenison, May 29, 1700, in *WMQ*, 2d ser., XIX (1939), 352–353.

5. *Charter, transfer, and statutes*, p. 15.

6. For a description of the Edinburgh library during the seventeenth century, see Sir Alexander Grant, *The story of the University of Edinburgh* (London: Longmans, Green and co., 1884), II, 168–184.

7. In his *Present state of Virginia* (London: J. Clarke, 1724), p. 26, Hugh Jones ascribes the design to Wren. For additional architectural data, see E. G. Swem, "Some notes on the four forms of the oldest building of William and Mary College," *WMQ*, 2d ser., VIII (1928), 217–307, and Marcus Whiffen, *The public buildings of Williamsburg* (Williamsburg, Va.: Colonial Williamsburg, inc., 1958), pp. 18–33.

8. J. W. Clark, *The care of books* (Cambridge: Cambridge university press, 1909), p. 137.

9. *Ibid.*, pp. 276–286.

10. *Vitruvius, the ten books on architecture*, tr. M. H. Morgan (Cambridge, Mass.: Harvard university press, 1926), p. 181.

11. Whiffen, *op. cit.*, p. 24.

12. S. E. Morison, *The founding of Harvard College* (Cambridge, Mass.: Harvard university press, 1935), p. 268. See also the account of seventeenth-century English college and university library financing in Albert Predeek, *A history of libraries in Great Britain and North America* (Chicago: American library association, 1947), pp. 17–18, 64–67.

13. E. A. Savage, *The story of libraries and book-collecting* (New York: E. P. Dutton & co. [n.d.]), p. 177.

14. The Nicholson catalogue has been transcribed and printed in Sadler Phillips' compilation of Fulham Palace records, *The early English colonies* (Milwaukee: Young churchman co., 1908), pp. 39–44.

15. *Journals of the House of Burgesses of Virginia, 1695 . . . 1702* (Richmond: [Colonial press], 1913), pp. 166–167.

16. [Nicholson], *op. cit.*, p. 35.

17. *Ibid.*

18. The full Nicholson catalogue, with expanded title entries, has been printed as an appendix to J. M. Jennings, "Notes on the original library of the College of William and Mary in Virginia," *Papers of the Bibliographical Society of America*, XLI (1947), 258–267.

19. Mentioned in the articles on Nicholson in *DAB* and in *The dictionary of national biography* (hereafter abbreviated to *DNB*).

20. *WMQ*, 2d ser., VIII (1928), 223.

21. For an account of "Blome's Bible," see *Notes and queries*, 2d ser., IV (1857), 310, 398.

22. "Dr. Bray's accounts . . . anno 1695 . . . anno 1699," Papers of the Society for the Propagation of the Gospel, Manuscript Division, Library of Congress.

23. L. B. Wright, *The first gentlemen of Virginia* (San Marino, Calif.:

Henry E. Huntington library, 1940; reprinted Charlottesville, Va.: University Press of Virginia, 1964), p. 126.

24. "Fourth scholar's speech," Francis Nicholson Papers, Library, Colonial Williamsburg, inc.

25. Mungo Ingles to Henry Compton, September 20, 1707, in *WMQ*, 2d ser., X (1930), 73–74.

26. "Fourth scholar's speech," previously cited.

27. James Blair to Thomas Tenison, February 12, 1700, in W. S. Perry, *Historical collections* ([Hartford]: Privately printed, 1870), I, 112–113.

28. James Blair to Thomas Tenison, May 29, 1700, in *WMQ*, 2d ser., XIX (1939), 352.

29. Thomas Tenison to Francis Nicholson, November 10, 1701, in *VMH&B*, XXII (1914), 248.

30. Thomas Hearne, *Remarks and collections* (Oxford: Oxford historical society, 1885–1921), I, 186.

31. Berkeley's *The lost lady; a tragycomedy*, for example, possessed sufficient merit to gain a place in Dodsley's collection of old plays.

32. For a full account of the peregrinations of this volume, see J. M. Jennings, "Rare book returned to library," *Alumni gazette [of] the College of William and Mary*, XIV (1947), 10–16.

33. *Op. cit.*, pp. 85–86.

34. Morison, *op. cit.*, p. 270. See also Predeek, *op. cit.*, p. 19.

35. Clark, *op. cit.*, p. 41.

36. Grant, *op. cit.*, I, 173.

37. Morison, *op. cit.*, p. 264.

38. *Op. cit.*, p. 91. Similar arrangements existed at English universities and colleges; see Predeek, *op. cit.*, p. 21.

39. "A modest reply to Mr. Commissary Blair's answer to my reasons for quitting the college," February 15, 1705, in *VMH&B*, IX (1901), 153.

40. [Nicholson], *op. cit.*, pp. 34–35.

41. Grant, *op. cit.*, I, 173.

42. D. M. Norris, *A history of cataloguing and cataloguing methods, 1100–1850* (London: Grafton & co., 1939), p. 148.

43. S. E. Morison, *Harvard College in the seventeenth century* (Cambridge, Mass.: Harvard university press, 1936), I, 294–296.

44. *Ibid.*, p. 295.

45. Whiffen, *op. cit.*, p. 33.

46. See official letter of notification sent by Governor Nott to the Board of Commissioners of Trade and Plantations, December 24, 1705, P.R.O., C.O. 5/1315, transcript in Manuscript Division, Library of Congress.

47. Mungo Ingles to Henry Compton, September 20, 1707, in *WMQ*, 2d ser., X (1930), 73–74.

48. *Executive journals of the Council of colonial Virginia* (Richmond: D. Bottom, 1925–46), III, 149.

49. Mungo Ingles to Henry Compton, September 20, 1707, previously cited.

50. *Ibid.*
51. Deposition of Mungo Ingles, September 20, 1707, Fulham Palace Manuscripts, Virginia, Box III, No. 41, transcript in Manuscript Division, Library of Congress.
52. *Ibid.*
53. *Ibid.*
54. See Swem, "Some notes on the four forms of the oldest building," *passim.*
55. Deposition of Mungo Ingles, September 20, 1707, previously cited.

CHAPTER THREE
Rebuilding the Book Collection, 1705–1743

1. Jones, *op. cit.,* p. 83.
2. Bounty warrant entered in "Old Queen's Warrant Book No. 17" (Treasury 52, Vol. 24, pp. 7–9, March 21, 1708/9), transcript in William and Mary College Papers, Folder 11A.
3. Governor Spotswood to Francis Fontaine, June, 1716, in R. A. Brock, *The official letters of Alexander Spotswood* (Richmond: Virginia historical society, 1882), II, 167.
4. "Proceedings of the visitors," March 26, 1716, *VMH&B*, IV (1896), 169.
5. *Ibid.,* June 20, 1716, p. 173.
6. *Charter, transfer, and statutes,* pp. 84–85.
7. Journal of the faculty, February 26, 1773, in William and Mary College Papers.
8. *Ibid.*
9. "Proceedings of the visitors," October 24, 1716, in *VMH&B*, IV (1896), 175.
10. *Ibid.,* June 13, 1716, p. 170.
11. Joseph Foster, *Alumni Oxoniensis* (Oxford: Parker & co., [n.d.]), early ser., I, 133.
12. For biographical data on Gibbon, see Gordon Goodwin, "John Gibbon," *DNB*, VII, 1135–1136.
13. Meriwether Stuart, "Textual notes on John Gibbon's manuscript notes concerning Virginia," *VMH&B*, LXXIV (1966), 476.
14. *Op. cit.,* pp. 83–84.
15. *Ibid.,* p. 90.
16. *Ibid.*
17. *Ibid.,* pp. 85–86.
18. *Charter, transfer, and statutes,* pp. 98–99.
19. Tyler, *College of William and Mary,* pp. 27–30.
20. *Op. cit.,* pp. 90–91.

21. *The charter, and statutes, of the College of William and Mary* (Williamsburg, Va.: Printed by William Parks, 1736), p. 113.

22. *Charter, transfer, and statutes*, p. 104.

23. James Blair to Edmund Gibson, August, 1732, Fulham Palace Manuscripts, transcript in William and Mary College Papers, Folder 9.

24. William Dawson to Edmund Gibson, August 11, 1732, *ibid.*

25. Adams, *op. cit.*, pp. 9–10.

26. "Instructions from the President and masters . . . to John Randolph . . . now bound for England," entered in Journal of the faculty, August 10, 1732.

27. President and masters to Micajah Perry, August 10, 1732, entered in Journal of the faculty, August 10, 1732.

28. "Instructions from the President and masters . . . to John Randolph."

29. W. W. Hening, ed., *The statutes at large* (Richmond: Franklin Press, 1820), IV, 429–433.

30. In 1745 (*ibid.*, V, 310–318); in 1757 (*ibid.*, VII, 133–134); and in 1769 (*ibid.*, VIII, 335–336).

31. Quoted from Wake's will in a letter of J. B. Stanford to Henry Wise, August, 1926, William and Mary College Papers, Folder 215.

32. James Blair to Edmund Gibson, July 17, 1738, in *WMQ*, 2d ser., XX (1940), 131–132.

33. James Blair to Edmund Gibson, May 12, 1739, in *WMQ*, 2d ser., XX (1940), 133.

34. For biographical data on Jones, see Goodwin, *op. cit.*, p. 282.

35. R. A. Brock, ed. *The official letters of Alexander Spotswood* (Richmond: Virginia historical society, 1882), I, xv–xvi.

36. William Gooch to Edmund Gibson, May 10, 1743, Fulham Palace Manuscripts, Virginia, Box I, No. 136, transcript in Manuscript Division, Library of Congress.

37. William Dawson to Edmund Gibson, August 11, 1732, Fulham Palace Manuscripts, transcript in William and Mary College Papers, Folder 9.

38. James Blair to Mr. Forbes, June 20, 1723, in Perry, *op. cit.*, I, 250–251.

39. *WMQ*, 1st ser., IX (1901), 61–62.

CHAPTER FOUR
Expanding the Book Collection, 1743–1776

1. See Dawson Papers, Manuscript Division, Library of Congress.

2. C. H. Canby, "A note on the influence of Oxford University upon William and Mary College in the eighteenth century," *WMQ*, 2d ser., XXI (1941), 243–247.

3. William Dawson to George Fothergill, August 18, 1747, Dawson Papers.

4. *Ibid.*

5. Predeek, *op. cit.*, p. 64.

6. Miscellaneous 1859 newspaper clippings in William and Mary College Papers, Folder 17.

7. Bursar's accounts, 1764–1770, Ledger B, and Bursar's accounts, 1770–1777, William and Mary College Papers.

8. Bursar's invoices, 1765–1771, William and Mary College Papers, Folder 260.

9. Journal of the faculty, January 25, 1742.

10. *Ibid.*, June 26, 1761.

11. Goodwin, *op. cit.*, p. 282.

12. Bursar's accounts, 1764–1770, Ledger B, p. 16.

13. Bursar's accounts, 1764–1770, Ledger B, and Bursar's accounts, 1770–1777.

14. See entries in Bursar's accounts, 1764–1770, Ledger B, p. 33.

15. Journal of the faculty, December 10, 1756.

16. William Dawson to Thomas Sherlock, July 27, 1750, Fulham Palace Manuscripts, transcript in William and Mary College Papers, Folder 9.

17. President and masters to Queen Victoria, March 19, 1861, draft in Journal of the faculty, March 19, 1861.

18. [Charles Campbell], "Notes," *Southern literary messenger*, III (1837), 237–238.

19. *Ibid.*

20. "Governor Dinwiddie's reply to the address of the president and masters," November 20, 1751, in R. A. Brock, ed., *The official records of Robert Dinwiddie* (Richmond: Virginia historical society, 1883), I, 5.

21. *Ibid.*, I, xiii.

22. John Sherwin to William Dawson, August 18, 1747, Dawson Papers.

23. Dawson Papers, *passim.*

24. William Dawson to Philip Bearcroft, July 12, 1744, Dawson Papers.

25. See Richard Lee Morton, "James Horrocks," *DAB*, IX, 235–236.

26. For biographical data on Henley, see G. P. Moriarty, "Samuel Henley," *DNB*, IX, 420–421, and Fraser Neiman's introduction to *The Henley-Horrocks inventory* (Williamsburg, Va.: Botetourt bibliographical society and the Earl Gregg Swem library, 1968), 5–9.

27. "The college to the estate of the late Mr. Horrocks, December 8, 1772," William and Mary College Papers, Folder 260; also reproduced in facsimile in *The Henley-Horrocks inventory* opposite p. 6.

28. See Jefferson's reflections on Small quoted in H. L. Ganter, "William Small, Jefferson's Beloved Teacher," *WMQ*, 3d ser., IV (1947), 504.

29. George P. Coleman, *The Flat Hat club and the Phi Beta Kappa society, some new light on their history* (Richmond: Dietz printing co., 1916), *passim.*

30. S. E. Morison, *Three centuries of Harvard, 1636–1936* (Cambridge,

Mass.: Harvard university press, 1936), p. 202.

31. See Goodwin, *op. cit.*, pp. 275-276, and Foster, *Alumni Oxoniensis,* later ser., II, 579.

32. Coleman, *op. cit.*, not paged.

33. The catalogue is printed in full in Coleman, *op. cit.*

CHAPTER FIVE
A Good Foundation to Improve Upon, 1776–1793

1. This is suggested by Canby in his "Note on the influence of Oxford University upon William and Mary College," previously cited.

2. Journal of the Virginia Convention, June 15, 1776, transcript made about 1839 or 1840 on behalf of the college by Richard Randolph, in William and Mary College Papers, Folder 13A.

3. *Ibid.*

4. Filed with transcripts from the journal of the Virginia Convention of June 15, 1776, in William and Mary College Papers, Folder 13A.

5. Journal of the faculty, April 9, 1777.

6. October 24, 1777, p. 3.

7. October 31, 1777, p. 3.

8. For biographical data on Madison, see G. McL. Brydon, "James Madison," *DAB*, XII, 182-184.

9. "Autobiography," in Paul Leicester Ford, ed., *The works of Thomas Jefferson* (New York and London: G. P. Putnam's sons, 1904), I, 75.

10. *Ibid.*

11. See "A bill for amending the constitution of the College of William and Mary, and substituting more certain revenues for its support," in Julian P. Boyd, ed., *The papers of Thomas Jefferson* (Princeton, N.J.: Princeton university press, 1950), II, 535-543.

12. For more details on these reforms, see Adams, *op. cit.*, pp. 36–41, and Tyler, *College of William and Mary*, pp. 60–62.

13. Journal of the faculty, December 29, 1779.

14. Boyd, *Papers of Thomas Jefferson*, II, 544-545.

15. Journal of the faculty, December 30, 1779.

16. Predeek, *op. cit.*, p. 26.

17. Journal of the faculty, May 20, 1780.

18. Claude Robin, *Nouveau voyage dans l'Amérique septentrionale, en l'année 1781* (Paris: Moutard, 1782), p. 108.

19. *Ibid.*

20. Journal of the faculty, May 20, 1780.

21. *Statutes of the University of William & Mary* (Richmond: Printed by Augustine Davis, 1792), pp. 6-7.

22. François-Jean de Chastellux, *Travels in North America in the years*

1780, 1781 and 1782, tr. Howard C. Rice, Jr. (Chapel Hill, N.C.: University of North Carolina Press for the Institute of Early American History and Culture, 1963), II, 444.

23. Journal of the faculty, November 25, 1783.

24. François Alexandre Frédéric La Rochefoucauld-Liancourt, *Voyage dans les États-Unis d'Amérique* (Paris: DuPont, 1799), IV, 291.

25. Comte de Vergennes to James Madison, June 8, 1785, transcript in William and Mary College Papers, Folder 215.

26. A detailed account of the gift to the University of Pennsylvania, together with a checklist of titles, is given in C. Seymour Thompson, "The gift of Louis XVI," *University of Pennsylvania library chronicle*, II (1934), 37–48, 60–67.

27. Howard C. Rice, Jr., in Chastellux, *op. cit.*, I, 310.

28. A set of Buffon's *Histoire naturelle*, donated by the king of France, was cited in contemporary newspaper accounts describing the losses sustained by the library in the conflagration of 1859. See clippings in William and Mary College Papers, Folder 17.

29. James Madison to comte de Vergennes, January 1, 1785, transcript in William and Mary College Papers, Folder 215.

30. George Tucker, *Letters from Virginia* (Baltimore: Fielding Lucas, Jr., 1816), p. 125.

31. Archibald B. Shepperson, *John Paradise and Lucy Ludwell* (Richmond: Dietz press, 1942), pp. 281–285.

32. Earl Gregg Swem to W. A. R. Goodwin, December 20, 1928, William and Mary College Manuscript Virginiana: Cities: Williamsburg, Folder 4A.

33. Journal of the faculty, July 12, 1783.

34. Jedidiah Morse to Ezra Stiles, December 30, 1786, Stiles Papers, Yale University Library.

35. Isaac A. Coles to Henry St. George Tucker, July 20, 1799, in *WMQ*, 1st ser., VIII (1899–1900), 158–159.

36. La Rochefoucauld-Liancourt, *op. cit.*, IV, 294.

37. Ezra Stiles to James Madison, July 12, 1780, Stiles Papers, Yale University Library.

38. James Madison to Ezra Stiles, August 1, 1780, Stiles Papers, Yale University Library.

39. James Thacher, *A military journal during the American Revolutionary war* (Boston: Cottons & Barnard, 1827), p. 270.

40. Louis Shores, *Origins of the American college library, 1638–1800* (Nashville, Tenn.: George Peabody college, 1934), p. 56.

41. Chastellux, *op. cit.*, II, 443.

42. Jedidiah Morse to Ezra Stiles, December 30, 1786, Stiles Papers, Yale University Library.

43. Edmund Randolph to Alexander Addison, July 29, 1792, Gratz Collection: Federal Convention: Case 1, Box 26, Historical Society of Pennsylvania.

44. La Rochefoucauld-Liancourt, *op. cit.*, IV, 290.

*The Library of The College of William and Mary
in Virginia, 1693–1793*

was composed, printed, and bound by
Kingsport Press, Inc., Kingsport, Tennessee.
The paper is Curtis Rag
and the type is Janson.
Design is by Edward G. Foss.